The New Nomads

Temporary Spaces and a Life on the Move

gestalten

Going Global
Thoughts on the New Nomad Phenomenon
by Shonquis Moreno

"To take advantage of serendipity, travel light," says designer Jan Chipchase. The globetrotting, problem-solving consultant is alluding to values—mobility, sustainability, well-being and (self-)discovery—that lie at the heart of a cultural shift that has been taking place over the past decade: The desire to break both into and free of urban life. We want to be urban, but not bound by the old codes of the city. We want to exploit a historically unprecedented degree of personal freedom and Chipchase himself is a case in point. His officeless office consults for clients on their home turf, setting up temporary research studios in more than 40 cities each year—in a Dubai skyscraper or on a mountainside in Myanmar. To travel light, he has even designed a durable, discreet duffel bag that he sells online. How Chipchase packs for the road—if he can't carry it, it doesn't come—says everything about the roads he hopes to travel: Wheeled luggage can only be wheeled over flat ground.

There are others like Chipchase, a tribe, a diaspora, or simply the like-minded who expect to shape the world instead of the world shaping them. We are the new nomads. Even in our railroad flats, studio apartments, and English basements, we are (re)turning to the life of the hunter-gatherer. We are merchants on the Silk Road trading in ideas, herders grazing the higher slopes in midsummer. And to be mobile, we slough the burden of our stuff, our places, our habits. We want to think our way out of the proverbial box and into a yurt or sailboat instead. We are not following the seasons, or the food sources, or the exotic spices, or the straight path. We are following serendipity.

We Will Be Ephemeral

In part, we are making the best of a serendipity forced upon us by circumstances and uncertainty. We may be living and working longer, but events of the day remind us that life is short. The generation coming up has seen the volatility of markets, faiths, politics, and our own nature and learned to take nothing for granted. Indeed, the nomad is an early adopter, a wayfinder on the frontiers of change. Historian Karl Scheffer once described Berlin as a city "condemned forever to becoming and never to being." But, in every city "becoming" has become the way we are. Some of us are getting comfortable with the notion that the journey—via plane or train, 60 Mbps or 20, T4 or Four Square, Ethernet, or Chat Roulette—is the destination.

Throughout history, every culture has represented itself through unique architecture—from the Colossus of Rhodes to the Roman Colosseum and Babylon's hanging gardens to the Crystal Palace. People lived and died in the same village, sharing common bloodlines, sometimes claustrophobic relationships, and with faith in the rewards that conformity would bring. Temples, palaces, the

Pyramids: these monuments expressed a society's power, established hierarchy, and showcased its innovations, while decorative arts movements formed around interior design, furnishings, and objects that conformed to these same ideas and ideals. In renaissance Italy, architecture was girt with ornament; by Adolf Loos's day, ornament had been declared a crime. In Manhattan, boardrooms scrape the sky, declaring the power of those who have risen to the top floor, with the panoramic and observing corner office representing highest authority. At times, however, the powers-that-be were questioned and a worm tucked into the code: Midcentury designers conceived of the open-plan office and modular furnishings to cultivate a more democratic environment (one that would only take hold much later). The rural poor had been pouring into cities where everyone was a stranger and the competition for resources fierce since the nineteenth century. By 2008, half of the world's population had migrated to urban areas. By 2050, urbanization is expected to consume more than 80 percent of the developed and 60 percent of the developing world. In the meantime, with the arrival of the Internet and the knowledge worker, hierarchies and geography have quickly begun to become irrelevant.

What does it say about our times then that structures and spaces now roll, hatch, unfurl, or fold up, open like spaceships, jewel boxes, or parasols, or simply disappearing into the landscape instead of dominating it? They are sheltering instead of muscle-bound, open instead of cellular. Now that technology has set us in motion, the urban nomad is influencing business, products, services, and the culture at large. In these pages, we see architects making structures that are mobile too: Tricycle House by People's Architecture Office and Sealander's caravan-yacht hybrid. You can carry Monica Forster's

inflatable Cloud room on your shoulder and flat-pack Adrian Lippman's FoldFlatShelter. They are facilitating our movement the way the airport sleeping pod by Arch Group does. Once the ultimate nomads, shipping containers like those used in Poteet Architects' Container Guest House are becoming permanent homes that speak to our need for compact spaces and more efficient living. Tengbom Architects gave Swedish university students everything they need to live well in their 10 Smart Square Meters dormitories. They are making spaces versatile and sustainable: a living room turns into a guest room, an office into a kitchen. Architects are designing open-plan multidisciplinary coworking offices that could be the seeds of a nomadic culture to come. The projects we see presented here, responding to the habits and habitat of the new nomad, are practical, human scale and experimental—but above all a product of their time.

Untethered From Tradition and Technology

Technology has made the flow of communication constant, business global, and friendships virtual. It promises to free us from workplaces and lets us reinvent them; improves industrial production but makes a luxury of the handmade; lets us micro-manage our relationships on-screen while making us appreciate a physical person across the table.

We are free to roam, literally, even when "roaming" is not free and long distance calls cost nothing on Skype. Magazine subscriptions come to our tablets wherever we are. Via Airbnb we **4**

the fastest growing demographic online and account for the bulk of web purchases. Whoever the new nomad is, he or she is creative but not necessarily an artist; she is a business consultant or social entrepreneur, a software developer, or a venture capitalist. He is someone like Dutchman Pieter Levels, who decided to launch 12 web start-ups in 12 months from as many cities—out of a single backpack. One of those start-ups was NomadList.io, which allows itinerant knowledge workers to browse world cities according to monthly cost of living, temperature, safety, and Internet connection speed among other criteria. Moving from being locked into a job to being constantly on the move is no longer creepy or criminal—it's cool.

now share beds and houses. We share and overshare everything on Twitter, Instagram, and Facebook, then fumble periodically with our privacy settings. We can tune in to Al-Jazeera from Sacramento and the BBC from Johannesburg. We can spend money from anywhere on the planet with PayPal, pay our Brooklyn bills and our American taxes from Istanbul with online banking, and soon digital currencies will make being a citizen of the world—and an identity thief—even easier.

On the one hand, privacy is dead: ambient intelligence will soon mine public space for "useful" information. Wearables like Jawbone UP3 track our most intimate biological data 24/7 and will soon provide prognoses too. We can use that data to make healthy lifestyle choices, but will someone else use it too? On the other hand: Long live privacy! A Frenchman has won the right in a European court to be digitally erased from Google's Internet search. Will it become possible to secure our messaging, our finances, and our reputations, or to become simply anonymous again?

Consider the fact that 50 percent of occupations may be redundant by 2030: print journalists, travel agents, lumberjacks, tax collectors, and even florists. In many fields, youth is privileged over experience and it is unlikely that workers will have only a single job in a lifetime. Once upon a time, our parents and grandparents held down a single job and owned a single house. Building a home bequeathed to the children was a testament to a family's success. In these more dynamic times, however, we are becoming renters and summer cottagers, building or commissioning architecture and micro-architecture to escape in even while standing still. We are bootstrappers and DIYers. We save money and make friends by living in close quarters with multiple roommates: Sleeping Pods by Sibling provide private bed-closet alcoves whose small size is offset by generous common space. Today we are more likely to construct a tree house outside Bergen for holiday use, take a caravan around the world for a few months, co-own a garden plot in Berlin, or erect a prefabricated starter home designed by Dutch construction company Heijmans on a vacant urban lot in less than 24 hours.

Out of the Box
Into the Cloud

Some people embrace these changes, some of us hate them, some love to hate them and others hate loving them. Nomadism is more a state of mind and a way of living than it is generational, gender-based, discipline-dependent, or geographical. In fact, the old demographic segments are not very useful anymore. The young and wealthy still adopt innovation the earliest, but age, gender, and income are losing their commercial relevance: The elderly make up

An Object in Motion Stays in Motion

Our increasing wirelessness at the personal level along with a relatively low cost of transportation has made nomadism possible. We are the frequent fliers. With a concurrent rise in the cost of living and real estate—according to Nomadlist.io, it now costs over 4,386 euros per month to live in Omaha, Nebraska but only 515 euros to live in Bangalore—nomads are looking for or creating alternate ways of living that emphasize fulfillment and well-being. Mobility demands architecture that is portable and versatile, with multifunctional objects and furnishings no matter how small. Sometimes the structure is actually mobile: It has wheels or wings or ambulatory legs like the Walking House by N55. Designers are experimenting with prefabricated and flat-pack homes, portable wooden kiosks and shacks, snow shelters, cantilevering hotels, and crocheted cabin concepts that allow users to explore the nomadic life at their leisure, sometimes while remaining in one comfortable spot.

In Jagnefalt Milton's thus-far conceptual project called A Rolling Masterplan, buildings move through the city of Andalsnes, Norway on new as well as existing railway tracks according to the seasons or events. Manuel Dominguez has imagined a nomadic city, dubbed Very Large Structure, that moves on caterpillar treads seeking optimal economic and physical conditions for its population. Room-Room by Encore Heureux + G. Studio is a hut pedaled around by bicycle that can be lain on three different sides, giving the occupant three different views out. Sometimes, we just want our space to be so convertible that it feels as if we have moved houses entirely. A hybrid of architecture and furniture, Liu Lubin's ziggurat-shaped Micro House in Beijing is made of three fiber-reinforced foam modules that are so light the inhabitant can flip them around to convert the living room into an office or bathroom. Urban planning is expediting local

transportation in original ways too: Glow-in-the-dark strips were embedded in a recently completed bike path connecting Eindhoven to Neunen in the Netherlands, charging during the day and then glowing for eight hours through the night.

There are more and more innovative ways through ever-smarter technology to bridge the distance that separates so many of us from our loved ones: Skype and Facetime offer some reconnection, allowing empty-nest parents to stay in touch with their children or friends to catch up across

time zones. The Good Night Lamp is a pair of lamps that form "a physical social network" even when separated by continents: When the Big Lamp is switched on, the Little Lamp is too, wherever or with whom it may be. Teledildonics are sex toys that let long-distance lovers interact in real-time via data-enabled devices. The OhMiBod Remote is a Wi-Fi-enabled app that allows the user to control his or her partner's "personal massager" from anywhere in the world while the Crave Duet Lux vibrator boasts a built-in USB connection for charging and 16GB of storage. Conversely, Eenmaal is a pop-up restaurant that only hosts people who are by themselves, billing itself as "an attractive place for temporary disconnection," demonstrating our growing interest in bridging the distance with our analog selves.

Nomadism is a commitment to opt out of the conventional "in the box" way of doing things. The old social contract is no longer delivering **6** on its promises, if it ever did: the American dream was just that. Instead it is a choice to opt into the one-person dinner table, the Cloud and the coffeehouse, or, say, the Ace Hotel lobby in Manhattan where on any given afternoon a dozen people of varying age can

be found working on their own or in small groups; the glow of open laptop lids looking much the same from Berlin to Boston and Beirut to Bloemfontein. Whether on the road, off-road, or momentarily still, nomads need spaces in which to physically (re)connect with the world and major cities have begun to offer similar environments in which members of the creative class may meet. H&M and Starbucks may be iconically global, but there is also a globalization of less corporate bodies. The independent coffee shop has a familiar air, if not face, from Omotesando to Marrakech. International events like TED Talks or TEDx or in the design world Pecha Kucha evenings, where each person presents 20 slides for 20 seconds each, contribute to the networking culture of the nomad. For members of this group it can be easier to navigate on that global level. They have more in common with people they meet at a design conference in Kuala Lumpur than with people living in the same building back "home."

En Route is the New Office

In Belle Epoque Europe, travelers touring the continent used to rent hotel rooms for weeks at a time. After all, it took 15 days on a steam-driven passenger liner to reach New York from London in the mid-nineteenth century and the first transatlantic flight was not until 1919: It took 23 days and 6 stops to make it. Today, with flights from Istanbul to New York clocking in at 10 hours, business has become increasingly international and economies entangled. As workers travel more frequently, en route has become the new office. Creatives are a case in point: for some, in-flight is one of the few opportunities to unplug and focus. New York designer Karim Rashid, who travels up to half the year, has said he can fill a 100-page sketchpad during a transatlantic flight. Artist Nina Katchadourian makes art using only materials she finds in-flight. Seat Assignment features a series of Old Master-like selfies called Lavatory Self-Portraits in the Flemish Style. They depict Katchadourian costumes from the seventeenth century in airline napkins and inflatable neck pillows.

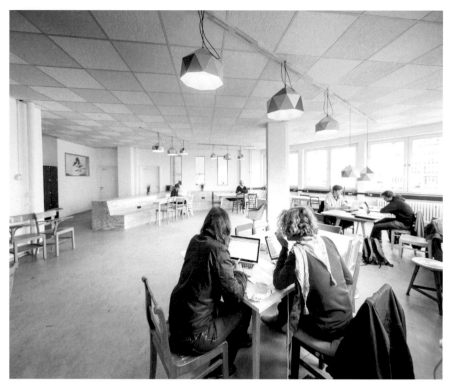

corporate ladder without putting other options to the test? The average American worker today stays at a job for just over four years; the youngest workers are expected to halve that. The new nomad knows that job-hopping can expedite her professional development, not retard it, and be more satisfying to boot. She tries on a variety of roles, titles, and workplaces, learns new skills and finds the best (read: most fulfilling) fit. Nomads are not waiting for the corporation to deem them of value; they are searching for their own and are willing to risk it all to do so—financial security, a nuclear family, two cars in the garage—which are not guaranteed anyway. They are not paying their dues. They are shopping.

When not in the air, we may increasingly work from compact home offices, but the nomad is also working on Jeju Island or in Chiang Mai (Nomadlist.io monthly cost of living and average connection speeds: 1,627/60 euros Mbps and 560/20 euros Mbps, respectively) or "wintering" in, say, Phuket where Thai visa policies are generous and visas free. Before she arrives, the nomad has mined contacts there or gotten the lay of the land from someone who has gone before her through social media. This allows her to prepare not only her infrastructure ahead of departure—renting a room or an out building from a local, maybe through Airbnb—but also a social network that is ready on arrival. These new friends can recommend a local yoga instructor or the strongest coffee, so that she is part of the community before even setting her watch to local time or setting up office—her laptop—in a cafe corner. When the nomad leaves, she leaves behind digital breadcrumbs for the next nomad to follow. It recalls the first half of the twentieth century when some of the finest writers and artists seemed nationless—to the point of fighting in other countries' wars—the difference being that Hemingway had to ship his typewriter to Madrid and Havana (on a ship) and lost a suitcase full of manuscripts along with all carbon copies on one short rail ride between Paris and Lausanne.

Now we have the freedom to move between workplaces or the freedom to not have a workplace at all. Millennials, along with nomads of earlier generations, will make up more than 75 percent of the global workforce by 2030. Businesses are beginning to understand that performance will become more important than attendance in the office, that giving workers opportunities to collaborate will be a requisite, and they have even begun to negotiate "unlimited" vacation time. And why climb an arduous

The Much More Bearable Lightness of Being

Experiences mean more but weigh less than things. Nomads are less concerned with the stuff they own and more with the stuff they can do or make. The minimalists slough their

belongings, selling them on Krrb or auctioning them on eBay, challenging themselves to slim down to fewer than, say, 100 items (and a couple of boxes of sentimental "baggage" stashed at their parents' houses.) In his book Stuffocation, British trendwatcher and author James Wallman points out that people who have lived through extreme scarcity are exceedingly frugal. It was the rise of the advertising industry in the mid-twentieth century that trained us in conspicuous consumption, which we are finally, Wallman argues, starting to turn into an experience economy instead.

As if to aid in this effort, some developers are hawking smaller apartments whose "intimacy" they compensate for by offering (sometimes pay-per-use) amenities and services that bring urban entertainment and convenience into the residential tower. One Istanbul developer commissioned a variety of public rooms for one building, including a cushion-clad Playstation room, a cigar den, a cinema, and a stargazing perch. Sloughing belongings to fit in these modern spaces is the path of least resistance. How much space and how much privacy do we need in an apartment we sleep in for only three months of the year? What do we need when we are only staying for a few days, a few weeks, or a season?

Some people will tell you that the things they value most live on their laptops or in the Cloud already. Even those who do not seek to be itinerant in any sense, can now digitize their music, photographs, accounting, and books. It becomes natural to live more lightly and more flexibly, to literally take up less space on the ground. The digital nomads who take these tools for granted are those who

pass seamlessly between city and countryside, coast to coast, and juggle multiple assignments at once: run a design-build studio between New York and Los Angeles, surf in Rio on the weekends, design shops in Sao Paulo during the week, or move to Tel Aviv from New York to cut on commute time to Milan manufacturers. Nomads do not want television. They text a lot and do not own a landline: Google's New York office shed its desk phones when it found that most of their employees were operating almost exclusively on their cellphones anyway.

Nomads are individualists, curious and open-minded, sophisticated and comfort-seeking, pan-cultural and multinational. They create work that is distinctly local while scouring the globe (and the Internet) for new ideas. They are romantics, idealists, and optimists who do not accept limits; instead they invent new ways around them and have the tools to do it. Think of the ambitious Seasteading Institute, co-founded by a former Google engineer and a PayPal co-founder, which is trying to establish floating cities that would serve as

facilitate person-to-person communication and collaboration instead of maintaining the chain of command. The idea that we will be phasing out of paper and boxes into more open-plan settings is not new. There have been stabs at this since midcentury: Gino Valle and Herbert Ohl's 1968 Multipli modular office furniture for Fantoni did this and more recently Konstantin Grcic's workplace collection for Vitra, which focuses on mobility, convertibility, and versatility. The idea is to enable coworkers to work together more

permanent, autonomous testing grounds and whose inhabitants would experiment with alternative social, governmental, and legal systems. Then there are the body hackers of Silicon Valley and beyond, bringing virtual values into the physical world: perfecting the human being by experimenting on themselves with everything from implanted magnets and supplements to modified Tibetan tea (in which yak butter and tea are replaced with Irish butter and coffee). They are not just thinking outside the box—for them, there is no box at all.

The Broken
Hierarchy and Sharing

Once upon a time that box was a cubicle, and if the cubicle was mostly public space, the desk in it was a personal object; now the near-obsolescence of both signals the decay of hierarchy (and has become a source of some confusion as 50-year-olds find themselves being managed by 27-year-olds). Increasingly, desks and offices must be designed to

organically, like a brain—all the synapses firing in reaction to each other—than a beehive, which is more mechanical.

A perfect picture of this flattening hierarchy is the "superdesk" designed by Los Angeles.-based architect Clive Wilkinson for New York Internet ad agency The Barbarian Group. In this 10 office, an endless desk forms the fabric of the whole interior—walls, desks, ceilings, conference rooms, and lounges. Having worked with TBWA/Chiat/Day and Google previously, Wilkinson designed an 3,35-meter-long work surface made of plywood and medium-density fiberboard that arches through the office, promoting flexibility and connecting 125 employees, including the chairman who works while standing (another growing trend, now that sitting is known as the new smoking.)

In coworking spaces, unrelated but thoroughly vetted creatives from various disciplines rent shared office space that tends to be furnished with more multiperson tables and sofas than desks and with labs and workshops as much as work surfaces. The Agora Collective is a community in Berlin based on diversity and social ties that features a laboratory kitchen, shared space for freelancing creatives, and collaborative artistic residencies. In a glass-walled, open-plan cabin in the woods designed by Raumlaborberlin, students of architecture, social and political science, economy, activism, art, and music came together to imagine the future of communal living. But coworking is also happening spontaneously in found locations: Breather is an app currently available in New York, Montreal, Ottawa, and San Francisco that allows users to locate unused urban spaces to rent for as little as 30 minutes and access them by way of the NFC keyless entry system.

Right now, however, co-working spaces, popping up around the globe, represent the prototype interior for the urban nomad. They offer

a variety of equipment, tools, and services to address the needs of diverse workers, whose like-mindedness draws them together as a tribe. More than any other environment, these may be the spaces in which the nomadic culture could coalesce and evolve into an active, identifiable demographic with common interests, methods, and goals. For now, nomadism may simply be a way of living and thinking, but the coworking spaces of today have the potential to become the labor unions and politically influential or activist bodies that will represent the globetrotting freelancers of the future. They are also the incubators of startups, social enterprises, etc.

Blurred Roles and Rituals

These changes entail not just the blurring of traditional roles and relationships but a blurring of activities, spaces, and spatial programs. In the public sphere, the hotel lobby has become the new living room, office hours are leisure time, and the office the new cultural hub. Fashion is the new uniform and textiles are armature. The rucksack contains an entire room with a view and airplanes are the new buses. The separation of domestic rooms according to function does not make much sense anymore either: The kitchen has morphed into the living room, the bed has become a desktop, and the bathroom a spa. What amenities does a living room need if the inhabitants conduct daily video conferences there? Graham Hill's Life Edited apartment, designed by two Romanian architecture students, converts radically to

fiteight rooms into 39 square meters: The living room and office become the bedroom. Ten stacking chairs and a telescoping dinner table are contained in a small cabinet, while a guest room, replete with bunk-beds, folds out of a gliding wall. Even when obsessively organized, it is all a little confusing, but nomads can live with that. In fact, chaos, miscegenation, and inversion are preferable. Glossy shelter magazines have been joined by publications like *Apartamento*, *Dirty Furniture*, and (online) *Freunde von Freunden* that are more relevant to the wider public than *Architectural Digest*.

Back to the Land

Though many nomads have come to the big city from somewhere less urban and find that they thrive there, they want to contain nature too. Literal or notional, the results are a hybrid of the hinterland and the cosmopolitan. Bivouac by Thomas Stevenson allows users to pitch a tent on city rooftops. Park(ing) Day, inaugurated in San Francisco in 2005 but now celebrated annually in cities worldwide, momentarily transforms metered parking spaces into public parks and art installations floored with Astroturf and furnished with lawn chairs.

At times, this journey back to nature occurs from the safety and comfort of home, at the community garden down the block, or in the co-ops that form around urban or indoor farming

projects. Suburban Tipi by John Paananen lets users set up a space of solitude in the living room. CAMP Daybed by Stephanie Hornig is a sleeping bag-like upholstery for the couch that makes a few minutes of reclining feel like a little journey.

Some city dwellers, however, want to leave city limits and slot back into nature momentarily (which may account for the wild popularity of tree houses in recent years.) Antoine by Bureau A is a hut camouflaged as a rock, portable by truck that fits into the landscape as if native to it. Likewise, the mirrored hut called Lookout by Process Craft may look man-made but it allows its occupant to disappear into the landscape in the very act of observing it. Professional escapists exist too, like Miscellaneous Adventures who host workshops with titles like Winter Camp or Woodland Woodcarving Skills. There is also Alastair Humphreys, who takes urbanites on mystery one-night micro-adventures which he bills as "a refresh button for busy lives." He calls it, not 9-to-5, but "5-to-9 thinking."

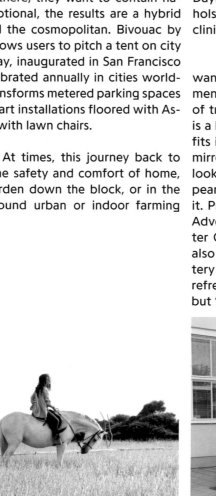

A Softer World

Will these cultural shifts free nomads to assume the burdens of a fraught world or will their kind—eternally leaving in pursuit of their own happiness—disperse and hunker down? New York designer Stephen Burkes of Readymade Projects is a nomad who is shouldering the burden. Though constantly on the move, Burkes synthesizes what he learns out in the world and back at home, and applies the results to commercially and artistically viable objects and environments. Synthesis and fusion may be the strongest creative forces wielded by the nomad, who responds to the proliferation of screens and gadgets by imbuing them with the handmade and the haptic and vice-versa. Burkes visits makers around the globe, learning their traditional methods and teaching them how to bring their skills to the contemporary international market. In the process, he creates—often soft, often woven—craft-influenced modern design for clients like Missoni, Moroso, and Roche Bobois. Any single Readymade product or environment is an amalgamation of cultural traditions, handcrafting techniques, and local or ad hoc materials. This means that while most of us are seeking shelter in a time of crisis

and uncertainty, the nomad is exposing himself to a world that may not be nearly as vast as the web, but which can sometimes feel that way.

"We are an unstitched society suffering from a lasting socio-economic crisis that has made us ferociously protective and egocentric," trend forecaster and curator Lidewij Edelkoort has said, using textiles and techniques like weaving, felting, knitting, and draping as metaphors and objects of comfort and safety. "It is time for mending and gathering, thus restoring the fabric of society: picking up the pieces and bringing them together in a patchwork of possibilities; a quilt of substance, able to absorb shock and fear."

In this sometimes fearful world, unburdened and embracing an unprecedented freedom of movement, will nomads ever stop searching for home, hoping to find it on a tide of serendipity? The answer is no, and yet home has become an idea more than a place, an idea that we can carry with us without even knowing it is there. It is a collection of memories, half-truths, and complete fictions that are the construction materials of an architecture we build, demolish and rebuild, renovate, and retrofit in our minds. It is a collection of experiences and people, not a collection of things. Unlike serendipity, home is something we make, not find. And it only becomes more precious and knowable if we leave it sometimes to go far, far away. ●

AARON MARET
Pocket Shelter

This tiny house on wheels represents a synthesis of thoughtful design and detail-oriented craftsmanship. Five years in the making, the modestly charming shelter functions as an experiment in alternative construction and living. The pitched roof home features reclaimed wood cladding that grants it a rustic quality and high level of durability. An intimate interior makes room for only the most essential elements of daily life. Freeing up excess clutter, expense, and maintenance, the compact home inspires its occupants to live within their means. Built on wheels, the little dwelling allows its residents the luxury of changing locations as the adventure of life unfolds.

14

ÁBATON
Portable House ÁPH80

This mobile dwelling provides charming, intimate quarters for two occupants. Easy to transport and able to be placed anywhere, the gabled cabin can be built for just 21,000 euros. The wooden home, clad in cement-board panels, enjoys a rare flexibility and responsiveness to the needs of its users. The gray panels shut tight to form an impenetrable fortress when on the move or during inclement weather. Otherwise, these panels swing open to welcome in the landscape all around. Sliding glass doors promote indoor/outdoor living, extending the modest floor plan into nature. Manufactured in eight weeks and installed in a single day, the tiny home comprises a shared living and kitchen space, a full bathroom, and a bedroom.

MAPA ARCHITECTS
Minimod

Flexible and prefabricated, this modular cabin allows its guests to relocate when the mood strikes. The compact and contemporary hideout welcomes a single occupant or couple for a memorable retreat framed by changing scenery. Sliding glass doors on two sides are paired with floor-to-ceiling windows that cap the two short faces of the structure. These generous apertures grant the modest layout an expansive feeling, inviting an immersive nature panorama to wrap around the dwelling. The sliding doors open onto an entry on one side and a sun deck on the other. Topped with a green roof, the mobile and expandable shelter integrates a kitchen, living, and sleeping area with a bathroom and shower tucked discreetly behind. With just a pane of glass separating the shower from the landscape beyond, guests enjoy the invigorating sensation of bathing in the great outdoors.

RAAAF - STUDIO FRANK HAVERMANS
Secret Operation 610

When aircraft Shelter 610 opens its ruthless doors, a black behemoth slowly drives out. The striking object revives the mysterious atmosphere of the Cold War and its accompanying terrifying weaponry. At an almost excruciatingly slow pace, the science fiction-esque artwork uses its caterpillar tracks to cross a seemingly infinite runway. The commanding and muscular object's constantly changing position in the serene landscape allows the visitor to experience the area and the history of the military airbase in a new and unexpected fashion.

A modular dwelling system enables occupants to live a peaceful nomadic life, moving slowly through the landscape or cityscape with minimal impact on the environment. The structure collects energy from its surroundings using solar cells. Sustainable and self-supporting, the elevated and geometric shelter also integrates a rainwater collection system, solar heated hot water, and a composting toilet system. A small wood-burning stove provides CO2-neutral heating. The unit forms various sizes of communities or mobile villages when additional units come together. Off the grid, the striking hideout remains independent from existing infrastructure and moves easily over terrains that one may find when taking the road less traveled.

Appearing as an occupiable boulder, a rugged shelter offers a minimalist habitat for simplified living in the Alps. Extending beyond the Swiss tradition of digging and carving the mountains for various dwellings, military infrastructure, and ski areas, this refuge also references the seminal book Bunker Archaeology written by Paul Virilio as well as the visionary sculpted works of Claude Parent and André Bloc. A luminous and understated plywood interior offsets the rugged exterior. This hybrid between sculpture and architecture can be picked up and transported from place to place on the bed of a truck—the ultimate rolling stone.

ANGRYBOVINE
Mobile Design Studio

A mobile home serves as the flexible work-space for a Colorado-based brand and design agency. Rejecting the corporate office culture, the founder opted for a solution that would bring his design practice closer to home. This fully retrofitted aluminum-trailer-turned-mobile-office stands just a few feet away from the owner's front door. The 28 square meters space holds a conference area and three workstations. Cheerful and bright, this creatively repurposed trailer highlights the possibilities for thinking and working outside the box.

JAY NELSON
Golden Gate 2

An efficient interior floor plan and a whimsical exterior shape define this mini electric camper car. Made with fiberglass, epoxy resin, plywood, glass, bike parts, and an electric motor, the handmade vehicle can drive 16 kilometers on a single charge at speeds of up to 32 kilometers per hour. The interior accommodates a kitchen with a sink, stove, cooler, and storage units as well as a toilet and bed with built-in storage. With all the controls consolidated in the steering wheel, the driver sits cross-legged while operating the vehicle.

BRAD FORD
Bulleit Frontier Whiskey Woody Trailer

An old fashioned trailer with wood siding hides a fully operational, world-class whiskey and bourbon bar inside. The vintage style of the exterior extends through the interior, boasting sleek leather furnishings, rich wood finishings handcrafted from reclaimed Bulleit Bourbon casks, and elegant glassware. A top-notch entertainment and sound system adds to the festive nature of this bar on wheels. The bar slides out of the hatch, welcoming lucky guests to grab a drink before the transient trailer moves on to the next location.

BRITISH STANDARD BY PLAIN ENGLISH
Shepherd's Hut

Fulfilling a longstanding wish of the company's creative director, a tiny shepherd's hut transforms into an idyllic extension of home. The cozy cabin kitchen introduces cupboards, a simple stovetop range, and shelving to form this charming and utilitarian cooking space. Perched on wheels, the mobile hut resides near both British Standard and parent company Plain English. Now used as a versatile and traveling showroom, the modest shelter inspires those with small spaces to think creatively while showcasing the quality of the cupboards and quirkiness of the brand.

30

BUREAU A
Ta đi Ôtô

Responding to the dense vernacular of Hanoi, this slender tower inspires a variety of uses and activities. The curious structure on wheels attaches to a bicycle to move through the city. Conceived as a support for different aspects of daily life, the tower becomes an ephemeral house one day and a vertical street food restaurant the next. The provocative structure with a playful pitched roof deviates from expectations and conventions. From a mini-concert hall to a poetry podium, the only barriers facing this structure are the limits of your imagination.

BUREAU A
Nomad

A caravan of trailers and tents temporarily repurposed the private gardens of the Musée du Quai Branly in Paris for a series of public programs. The charming medley of transient structures, carpets, and stools results in an informal architecture derived from the assemblage of recycled and transformed objects. Domesticating and appropriating the garden for public use, the lightweight and mobile installation features five informal settlements. These different groupings meander across the grounds and host a variety of events and refreshment options. Rethinking existing relationships between public and private spaces, the inviting caravan transforms the outdoors into a shared living room for impromptu gatherings.

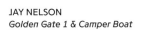

JAY NELSON
Golden Gate 1 & Camper Boat

By land or by sea—this innovative designer has a solution for everyone. These two nomadic structures rethink the design of life lived on the move. The first idiosyncratic dwelling consists of a rounded shelter made from plywood, plexiglass, and bicycle parts. Outfitted with geometric windows, an electric motor, and a surfboard rack, the tiny hideout on wheels inspires a fluid and mobile approach to daily life. The second structure, a charming boat prototype made of plywood and fiberglass, was designed to travel up the lagoon and back for small surfing expeditions.

KEVIN CYR
Home In The Weeds

A personal reaction to the economic down-turn, this micro camper acts as a safe haven for weathering the recession and other worst-case scenarios. Themes of mobility, concealment, and protection influence the design. Part of a larger exhibition on flexi-ble living, this tag-along shelter represents the most romantic prototype. The small hideout on wheels is towed by a vintage three-speed Raleigh bicycle and stocked with items reminiscent of an idyllic child-hood camping trip. Simple to transport, the shelter inspires a fluid and responsive approach to our ever-changing context.

SIGNBUSS

HEJ!
VÄLKOMMEN TILL MIN DESIGNBUSS. HÄR INNE BOR OCH ARBETAR JAG SOM
GRAFISK DESIGNER. JAG FÖRSÖKER TA MIG FRAM GENOM SVERIGE GENOM ATT
BYTA TJÄNSTER MED FOLK; JAG DESIGNAR NÅGOT TILL DIG OCH FÅR NÅGON
TJÄNST ELLER VARA TILLBAKA.

VÄLKOMMEN IN PÅ EN KAFFE SÅ KAN VI PRATA MER. OM JAG INTE ÄR HÄR SÅ
KAN DU RINGA MIG PÅ 0707–491312 ELLER BESÖK WWW.ERIKSDESIGNBUSS.SE

/HÄLSNINGAR ERIK

[SYSTEMTEXT]

ERIK OLOVSSON
Erik's Design Bus

This experimental mobile design studio features a print shop and photo studio, where the designer/owner can produce locally in a small edition. Opting not to be fixed to an urban area, the playful vehicle painted in colorful graphics challenges business and work conventions as it moves through the countryside. Studying how value varies depending on geographic location and demographic, the mobile work station barters design services for other services and products as an alternative economy. The eye-catching mobile-home-turned-workspace breaks down conventions and barriers between work and travel, customer and product.

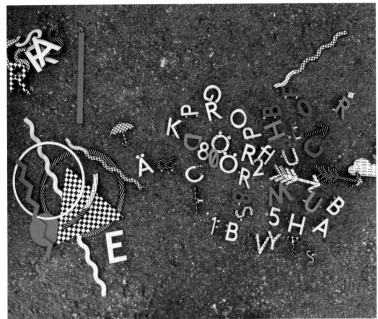

DANIEL PALMA
Tell a Story

A new, mobile bookshop travels through the streets of Lisbon to expose the best of Portuguese literature to the millions of tourists that visit the city each year. From Pessoa to Peixot, Queiroz to Sousa Tavares, Torga to Lobo Antunes, and Sophia to Saramago, the charming retro camper enables an authentic experience of Portugal through the eyes of the country's most influential writers. A simple bookshelf, matching the color palette of the vehicle, showcases a selection of Portuguese authors and invites visitors to take a seat, browse through the rich literary history, and even contribute a story of their own.

ONCE UPON A TIME THERE WAS
A COUNTRY BORN WITH THE GIFT OF WRITING
AN AUTHOR THAT WANTED TO TELL A STORY
A BOOK THAT WANTED TO BE READ
A TOURIST THAT DID NOT SPEAK PORTUGUESE
AND A BOOKSHOP THAT DID NOT KNOW
HOW TO REMAIN IN SAME PLACE.
ALL OF THEM JOINED TOGETHER
AND WROTE A NEW STORY.

41

MICHAEL SCHLÖSSER & MARION SEUL
BaseCamp Young Hostel Bonn

Sixteen vintage caravans form a playful indoor camping ground. The unique hostel's thematic design comprises two night sleepers, four American airstreams, and a handful of other oddities inside a former storage facility turned Caribbean campground. Whether approached as a hotel, a hostel, or a quirky installation, the compound maintains an infectiously upbeat spirit. Designed to fulfill the needs of backpackers, students, adventurers, and those seeking a more unconventional place to stay, the one-of-a-kind experience combines comfort with a retro vibe to produce a memorable interpretation of camping in the great indoors.

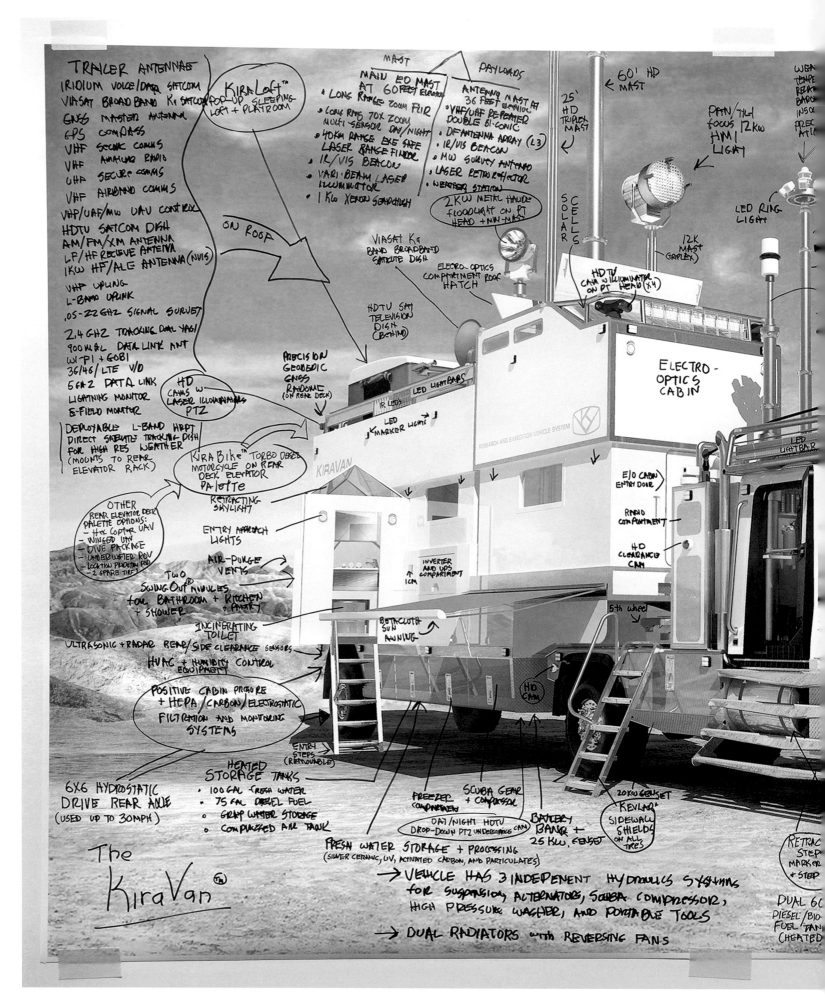

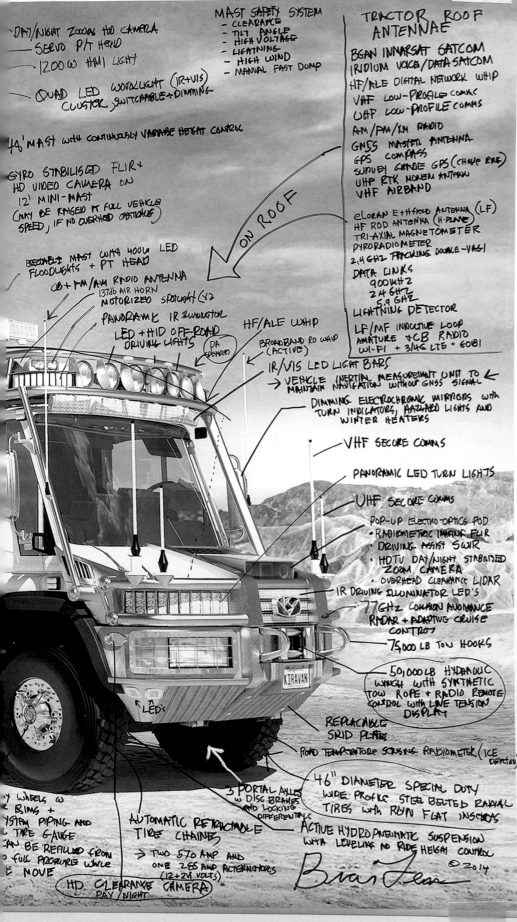

APPLIED MINDS, LLC
KiraVan Expedition Vehicle

A large-scale expedition system makes seldom visited places with untouched natural beauty accessible for over-land exploration, still photography, film production, and scientific research. The caravan maximizes both space and performance. Principal design goals extend flexibility and modularity. Minimizing crew workload while increasing their situational awareness, the unit applies a light touch to the natural environment. The expedition vehicle also provides more kid-friendly spaces. The utilitarian and industrial camper organizes a series of interrelated places to work, play, interact, and carry out personal research and discovery.

MAST SAFETY SYSTEM
- CLEARANCE
- TILT ANGLE
- HIGH VOLTAGE
- LIGHTNING
- HIGH WIND
- MANUAL FAST DUMP

TRACTOR ROOF ANTENNAE

- DAY/NIGHT ZOOM HD CAMERA
- SERVO P/T HEAD
- 1200W HMI LIGHT
- QUAD LED WORKLIGHT (IR+VIS) CLUSTER, SWITCHABLE+DIMMING

48' MAST WITH CONTINUOUSLY VARIABLE HEIGHT CONTROL

GYRO STABILISED FLIR + HD VIDEO CAMERA ON 12' MINI-MAST (MAY BE RAISED AT FULL VEHICLE SPEED, IF NO OVERHEAD OBSTACLE)

ON ROOF

DEPLOYABLE MAST WITH 400W LED FLOODLIGHTS + PT HEAD
CB+FM/AM RADIO ANTENNA
137db AIR HORN
MOTORIZED SPOTLIGHT (X2)
PANORAMIC IR ILLUMINATOR
LED + HID OFF-ROAD DRIVING LIGHTS
PA SPEAKERS

BGAN INMARSAT SATCOM
IRIDIUM VOICE/DATA SATCOM
HF/ALE DIGITAL NETWORK WHIP
VHF LOW-PROFILE COMMS
UHF LOW-PROFILE COMMS
AM/FM/XM RADIO
GNSS MASTER ANTENNA
GPS COMPASS
SURVEY GRADE GPS (CHIVE RNG)
UHF RTK MODEM ANTENNA
VHF AIRBAND

eLORAN E+H FIELD ANTENNA (LF)
HF ROD ANTENNA (H-PLANE)
TRI-AXIAL MAGNETOMETER
PYRORADIOMETER
2.4 GHz TRACKING DOUBLE-YAGI
DATA LINKS
    900MHz
    2.4 GHz
    5.9 GHz
LIGHTNING DETECTOR
LF/MF INDUCTIVE LOOP
AMATURE + CB RADIO
WI-FI + 3/4G LTE + GOBI

HF/ALE WHIP
BROADBAND RO WHIP (ACTIVE)

IR/VIS LED LIGHT BARS

VEHICLE INERTIAL MEASUREMENT UNIT TO MAINTAIN NAVIGATION WITHOUT GNSS SIGNAL

DIMMING ELECTROCHROMIC MIRRORS WITH TURN INDICATORS, HAZARD LIGHTS AND WINTER HEATERS

VHF SECURE COMMS

PANORAMIC LED TURN LIGHTS

UHF SECURE COMMS

- POP-UP ELECTRO-OPTICS POD
- RADIOMETRIC IMAGING FLIR
- DRIVING ASSIST SWIR
- HDTV DAY/NIGHT STABILISED ZOOM CAMERA
- OVERHEAD CLEARANCE LIDAR
IR DRIVING ILLUMINATOR LED'S
77GHz COLLISION AVOIDANCE RADAR + ADAPTIVE CRUISE CONTROL
75,000 LB TOW HOOKS

50,000LB HYDRAULIC WINCH WITH SYNTHETIC TOW ROPE + RADIO REMOTE CONTROL WITH LIVE TENSION DISPLAY

REPLACABLE SKID PLATE
ROAD TEMPERATURE SENSING RADIOMETER (ICE DETECTION)

46" DIAMETER SPECIAL DUTY WIDE PROFILE STEEL BELTED RADIAL TIRES WITH RUN FLAT INSERTS

LED's

ALLOY WHEELS W RIMS + SYSTEM PIPING AND TIRE GAUGE CAN BE REFILLED FROM FULL PRESSURE WHILE ON MOVE

AUTOMATIC RETRACTABLE TIRE CHAINS

3 PORTAL AXLES W DISC BRAKES AND LOCKING DIFFERENTIALS

ACTIVE HYDROPNEUMATIC SUSPENSION WITH LEVELING AND RIDE HEIGHT CONTROL

TWO 570 AMP AND ONE 255 AMP ALTERNATORS (12+24 VOLTS)

HD CLEARANCE CAMERA DAY/NIGHT

© 2014

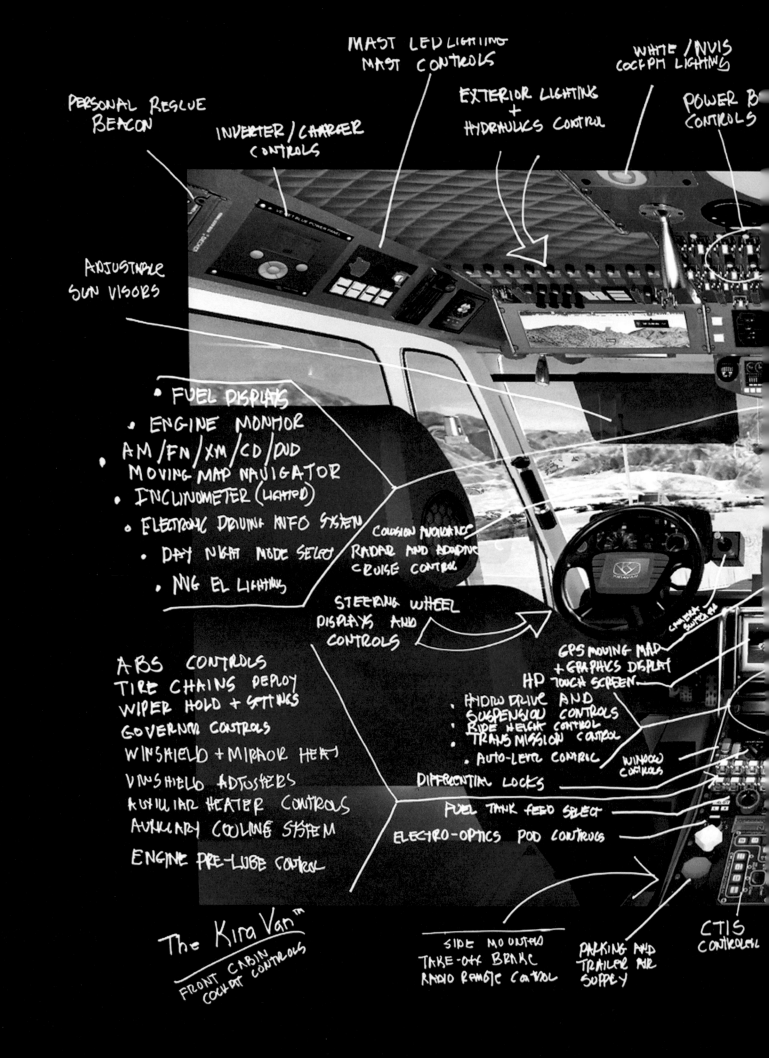

PERSONAL RESCUE
BEACON

MAST LED LIGHTING
MAST CONTROLS

WHITE / NVIS
COCKPIT LIGHTING

EXTERIOR LIGHTING
+
HYDRAULICS CONTROL

POWER B
CONTROLS

INVERTER / CHARGER
CONTROLS

ADJUSTABLE
SUN VISORS

• FUEL DISPLAYS
• ENGINE MONITOR
• AM/FM/XM/CD/DVD
  MOVING MAP NAVIGATOR
• INCLINOMETER (LIGHTED)
• ELECTRONIC DRIVING INFO SYSTEM
• DAY NIGHT MODE SELECT
• NVG EL LIGHTING

COLLISION AVOIDANCE
RADAR AND ADAPTIVE
CRUISE CONTROL

STEERING WHEEL
DISPLAYS AND
CONTROLS

GPS MOVING MAP
+ GRAPHICS DISPLAY
HP TOUCH SCREEN
• HYDRO DRIVE AND
  SUSPENSION CONTROLS
• RIDE HEIGHT CONTROL
• TRANSMISSION CONTROL
• AUTO-LEVEL CONTROL

WINDOW
CONTROLS

ABS CONTROLS
TIRE CHAINS DEPLOY
WIPER HOLD + SETTINGS
GOVERNOR CONTROLS
WINSHIELD + MIRROR HEAT
WINSHIELD ADJUSTERS
AUXILIAR HEATER CONTROLS
AUXILIARY COOLING SYSTEM
ENGINE PRE-LUBE CONTROL

DIFFERENTIAL LOCKS

FUEL TANK FEED SELECT

ELECTRO-OPTICS POD CONTROLS

CTIS
CONTROLS

The KiraVan™
FRONT CABIN
COCKPIT CONTROLS

SIDE MOUNTED
TAKE-OFF BRAKE
RADIO REMOTE CONTROL

PARKING AND
TRAILER AIR
SUPPLY

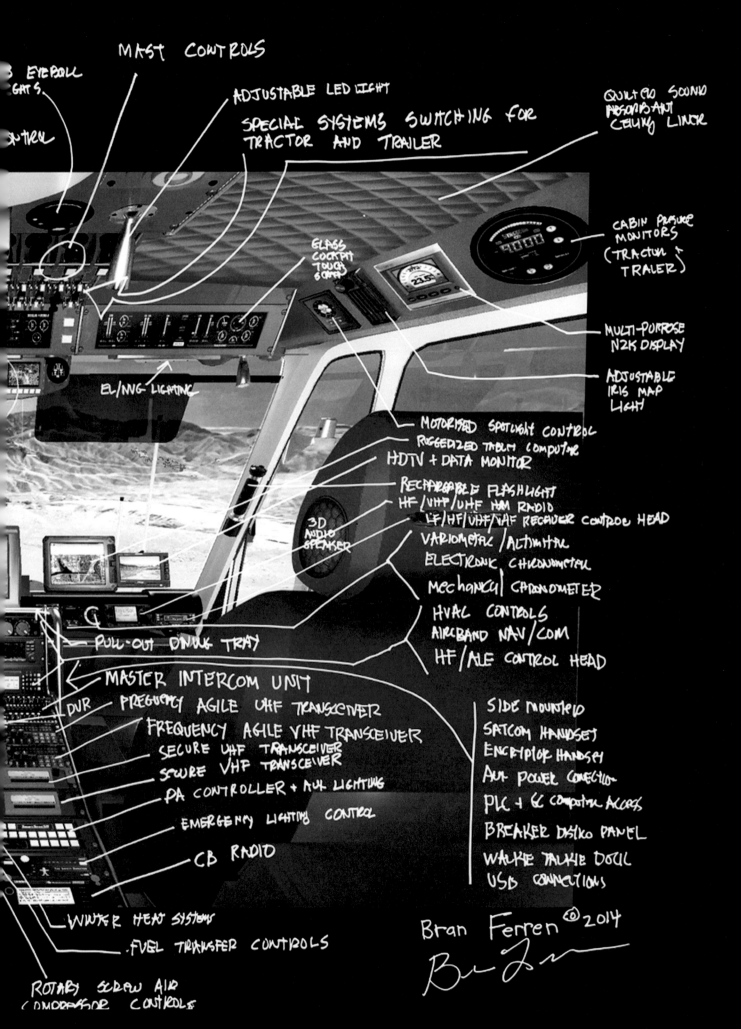

MAST CONTROLS

3 EYEBALL IGHTS.

NTRL

ADJUSTABLE LED LIGHT

SPECIAL SYSTEMS SWITCHING FOR TRACTOR AND TRAILER

QUILTED SOUND ABSORBANT CEILING LINER

GLASS COCKPIT TOUCH SCREEN

CABIN PRESSURE MONITORS (TRACTOR & TRAILER)

MULTI-PURPOSE N2K DISPLAY

ADJUSTABLE IRIS MAP LIGHT

EL/NVG LIGHTING

MOTORISED SPOTLIGHT CONTROL

RUGGEDIZED TABLET COMPUTER

HDTV + DATA MONITOR

RECHARGABLE FLASHLIGHT

HF/VHF/UHF HAM RADIO

LF/HF/UHF/VHF RECEIVER CONTROL HEAD

VARIOMETER/ALTIMETER

ELECTRONIC CHRONOMETER

MECHANICAL CHRONOMETER

HVAC CONTROLS

AIRBAND NAV/COM

HF/ALE CONTROL HEAD

3D AUDIO SPEAKER

PULL-OUT DINING TRAY

MASTER INTERCOM UNIT

DVR FREQUENCY AGILE UHF TRANSCEIVER

FREQUENCY AGILE VHF TRANSCEIVER

SECURE UHF TRANSCEIVER

SECURE VHF TRANSCEIVER

PA CONTROLLER + AUX LIGHTING

EMERGENCY LIGHTING CONTROL

CB RADIO

SIDE MOUNTED

SATCOM HANDSET

ENCRYPTOR HANDSET

AUX POWER CONNECTION

PLC + 6G COMPUTER ACCESS

BREAKER DISKO PANEL

WALKIE TALKIE DOCK

USB CONNECTIONS

WINTER HEAT SYSTEMS

FUEL TRANSFER CONTROLS

ROTARY SCREW AIR COMPRESSOR CONTROLS

Bran Ferren ©2014

ABERRANT ARCHITECTURE
Roaming Market

Created for Lower Marsh Market in Waterloo, the mobile structure can be moved to different sites and unfolded into a multi-functional market stall. This experimental project features a covered seating area with a built-in chessboard and a stage on the roof for hosting live events and performances. The design draws inspiration from a number of historical precedents and idiosyncratic structures found in the area. Reminding visitors of the region's long tradition with mystics and fortune-tellers, a giant chicken sign at the top of the structure references the chickens used to tell fortunes during Roman times. The stall behaves as a platform that accommodates an annual program of events and shared experiences for the contemporary market. Reflecting the unique character and atmosphere of the present within a historical framework, the new stall marks the next step in the Lower Marsh Market's evolving story.

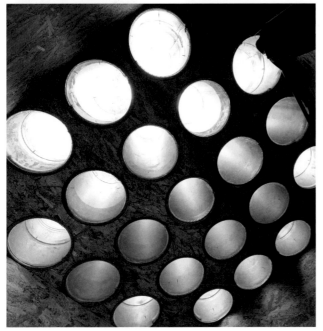

ABERRANT ARCHITECTURE
Tiny Travelling Theater

Towed by a VW split screen camper, an eye-catching, crimson-red mobile theater hosts an audience of up to six people at a time for a series of intimate one-off performances. These events, ranging from plays and comedy to live music, explore the intense emotion inherent in such intimate live performances. The unusual design, a nod to the Small-Coal-Man's Music Club created by Thomas Britton in 1678, integrates a number of quirky attributes from the original venue. A coal scuttle roof, referencing Britton's former profession and his concert hall's prominent organ, filters dappled light into the auditorium. Inspired by small one-on-one spaces, such as a confessional booth or a peepshow, audience members must duck to enter and are encouraged to join in the performances. A large sound funnel gives passersby a small taste of the acts occurring within, while folding tables and ice buckets form an impromptu bar outside for guests to enjoy a pre and post-performance drink.

ENCORE HEUREUX + G.STUDIO
Room-Room

This bright yellow mobile housing unit addresses the needs of our international homeless population. Designed with climatic, social, and economic considerations in mind, the lightweight shelter proves strong, safe, and affordable.

The ergonomic, thermally efficient, and easily transportable dwelling offers the largest of the smallest berth as well as the first room of an intended future dwelling. The multi-purpose object encourages a number of adaptive uses and orientations.

Whether hooked on to the back of a bicycle or pushed like a cart by hand, the pragmatic and inventive shelter empowers the homeless to live with flexibility as they navigate natural and social shifts in the environment.

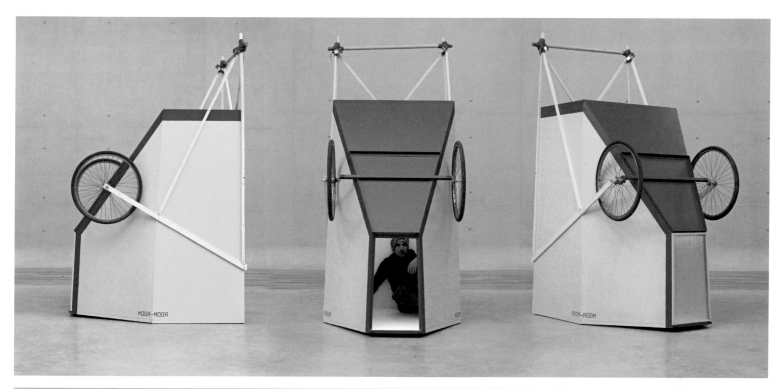

PEOPLE'S ARCHITECTURE OFFICE
Tricycle House

Embracing the temporary relationship between people and land, a home moved by tricycle develops a sustainable and affordable solution for single-family housing. Easily navigating the crowded streets of metropolitan China, the tiny shelter occupies parking lots at night and traffic jams by day. The entire house, made from scored and folded polypropylene plastic, supports the novel concept of living while moving. Indoor facilities include a sink and stove, a bathtub, a water tank, and furniture that can transform from a bed to a dining table or counter top. Reducing private living to the smallest footprint, the nomadic system promotes sustainable living by taking advantage of public resources. Public parks replace personal gardens, public toilets replace private toilets, parking spaces replace land ownership, and the translucent exterior keeps the interior illuminated with the sun by day and street lamps by night.

PAUL ELKINS
Bicycle Camper

When Paul Elkins was laid off from his job, he decided to travel across the United States. Rich in time but poor in transport and funding for lodging, he designed a discreet mobile pod from the six foot-long bed of his Toyota truck and canopy. The resulting nondescript white shelter hitches on to his bicycle, following along on his seven week coast to coast adventure. A battery operated hot wire charges his cell phone, radio, TV, and lights. Appearing to be a storage unit, the camper allowed him to sleep undetected in rest stops, truck stops, and neighborhoods across the country.

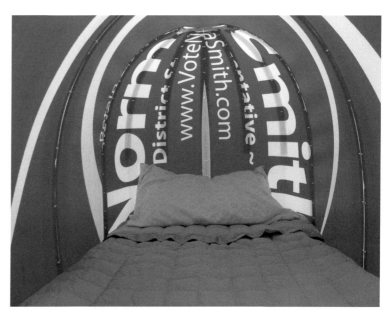

This mobile publishing platform generates, prints, binds, and distributes magazines on the spot. Inspired by Bruce Sterling's statement that "events are the new magazines," the portable kiosk produces a physical record of the fleeting aspects of physical interactions and electronic debris generated by event culture. The magazine's production plays on our shared fear of missing out. The performative process investigates the encounter between a centuries-old tradition of experimental publishing, the rising influence of machine intelligence in media, and the craving for instant gratification produced by real-time technologies. Background noise, audience size, and the intensity of social media inform the final output, creating both moments of density and voids of activity. In true Dadaist spirit, the project aims less at precise documentation than at alternative methods of representing ongoing events.

56

TILLY BLUE
The Travel Collection

A bespoke range of travel inspired furniture connects traditional woodworking ideals with conceptual design. The collection offers functionality and innovative variation on space-saving products. Each piece folds away into an easy to carry mobile version that resembles carry-on luggage. Taking inspiration from the spaces we occupy, the simple but pragmatic designs integrate markings, textures, colors, and shapes from the landscapes we live in and apply them as surface patterns on the various furniture pieces. This subtle contextual reference stimulates engagement and a sense of adventure in everyday life.

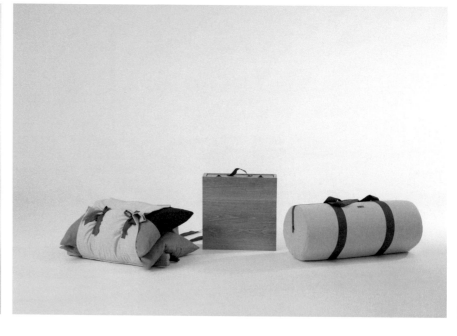

LEHMAN B
Supertramp

Exploring the practicality of micro-sized living, this shelter on wheels roams the urban streets of London. The basic cube, made from translucent fabric, latches on to a bicycle driven from one location to another. Inspired by a more minimal, fluid, and socially aware approach to future urban living, the project promotes braver and more authentic dwelling models. Enjoying an ever-changing scenery, fold-up panels introduce points of egress and windows into the small but bright space. Perhaps a symbolic commentary on the challenges of nomadic living, the project reached its abrupt end when it was stolen and never found again.

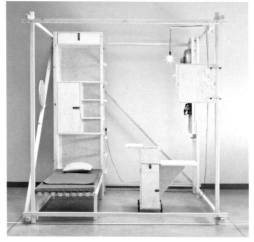

CHMARA.ROSINKE
2,5³

Influenced by the revolutionary modular and mobile living structures prototyped in the 1960s and 1970s, a minimalist living cube explores the limits of what people can live without. This paired-down housing solution reflects on the rise of contemporary nomadism and its implications on consumerism. The compact living space, a reinterpretation of the 1970s Living Cube by Papanek & Hennessey, highlights the important role that technology, notebooks, and smartphones now play in shaping our residential spaces. The multifunctional cube consists of a desk that can morph into a kitchen, a rolling cupboard that unfolds into an eating table for two, a bed, a closet, a mirror, and a drawer. A special chair, designed for the height of the kitchen and desk, folds to allow occupants to climb on top of the cube and enjoy a different view or read a book. The simple, wooden, and nomadic structure can be installed in an hour and closed off with textiles to add levels of privacy as needed.

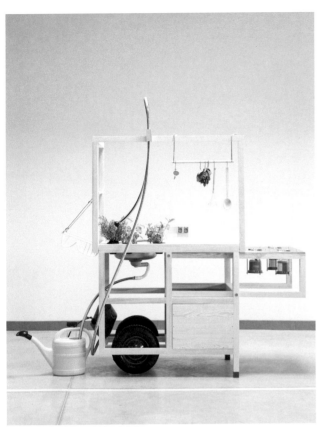

CHMARA.ROSINKE
Mobile Hospitality

This hybrid wheelbarrow kitchen roams from place to place supported by a table and 10 folding stools. At each location, the informal public space spontaneously invites passersby to grab a seat, socialize, and enjoy a meal. The formal language of the light wood unit retains an understated simplicity through its streamlined yet rudimentary design. This self-initiated urban activator utilizes the tiniest of footprints to achieve a delightful and lasting social experience. Here today and gone tomorrow, the unpretentious and welcoming mobile dining cart lingers in the collective memories of its guests.

FABRICA
Next Cabane

This project begins with a simple, foldable hut-like structure made of wooden slats found in a flea market in the north of Scotland. The hideout, originally covered with a tarpaulin, was used as a shelter for anglers. Now in its sixth iteration, this stripped-down mobile room installation develops temporary solutions for staging symbolic and protective spaces. The cabin functions as a place of work or play, or as an exhibition venue. As an enclosed space, the structure enables a more conscious perception of a given place and its characteristic materials, forms, and structures.

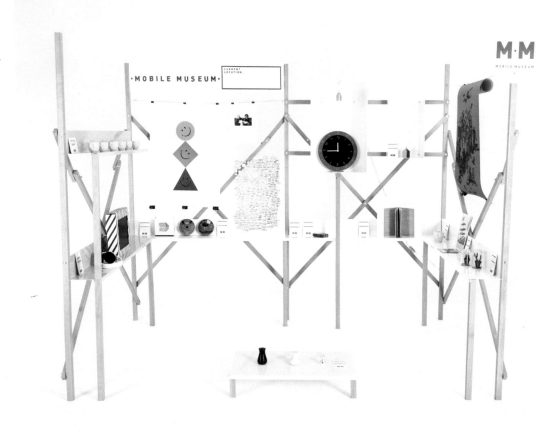

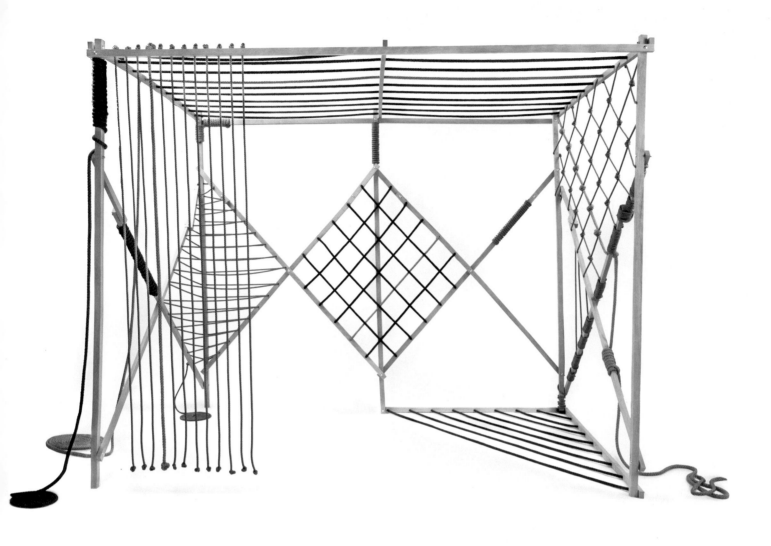

Temporary Architecture
by Werner Aisslinger

Designer Werner Aisslinger prides himself in working across mediums. The Berlin-based Studio Aisslinger handles projects encompassing everything from product and industrial design to art installations, interior design, and full-scale architecture prototypes. Many of Aisslinger's projects speculate on the future of the contemporary home and develop solutions for nomadic living within a compact, elegant, and consistent framework.

As space becomes an increasingly scarce commodity, designers must embrace ur-

Loftcube's unique ability to occupy the thousands of unused square meters on the rooftops of a city's skyline activates a previously untapped real estate market. Behaving as an independent addition to the existing high-rise context, the "UFO with legs" offers a bright, flexible, and transient model that can grow into a new vernacular for rooftop communities down the line.

The Loftcube currently comes in four sizes ranging between 30 and 82 square meters with prices starting at 100,000 euros. Still in limited production, Aisslinger acknowledges that the current

ban density and develop adaptive responses that do more with less. Loftcube, Aisslinger's modular and mobile housing solution, continues to receive international attention due to its foresight and pragmatism. The futuristic exterior and retro interior, reminiscent of famous historical prototypes by the likes of Buckminster Fuller and Jean Prouve, address a more current market through a distinctly urban approach.

price tag limits the clientele to exclusively high-end customers and hotels. However, his plans for serial production will decrease the cost dramatically and make the Loftcube a viable housing alternative for a broader market. Intentionally standing out against its generally banal surroundings, the striking nomadic dwelling can move from place to place, roof to roof, and city to city. Inside, the compact layout balances social spaces with privacy considerations. Each incarnation stands as an appealing reminder of the vast potential in repurposing the extant spaces at the top of our metropolises.

Whether working on an installation or a product, Aisslinger's designs have lasting value that lingers in the minds of visitors or passes down through generations of consumers. His intention for both his more temporary and permanent projects is

to encourage users to forge connections between the design and their daily life. "The ultimate design value is a long product half-life," Aisslinger explains. "Sustainability is maximized when objects are not thrown away and replaced but used for generations." The studio's constant research of new and sustainable materials and production processes results in projects with sophisticated aesthetic agendas and low carbon footprints.

Engaging with many of the social problems of our time, the studio also explores design solutions for the future of food production. Some of these scenarios were featured in Aisslinger's illuminating "Home of the Future" exhibition in Berlin. This exhibition included novel alternatives for kitchen farming, urban farming, and upcycling processes. A walk through the exhibition revealed a systematic rethinking of typical residential spaces from the kitchen and living room to the bathroom. The imaginative alternatives on display broke with the conventions and expectations people have for a home. Unlike installations from the 60s and 70s where the future was always imagined in a space travel context, this exhibition focused on current problems facing our society. Aisslinger covered both a car and the entire façade of the museum in a colorful fabric skin to promote the concept of upcycling. "Changing the visual setup [of cars or buildings] from time to time is less complex than replacing them and consumes less CO_2," Aisslinger argues. The exhibition also presented a green bath that uses special fabrics to absorb water vapor and transfer it to an irrigation system for plants.

Aisslinger's work fights against the trend of increasing complexity in design. Instead, his approach to architecture and the design process focuses more on natural materials and simplicity. "Future architectural setups have to care about topics like communal interaction, sharing, multi-generational housing, integration of urban indoor farming, and nomadic buildings," he points out. As communication quickens and becomes increasingly tied to technology and a nomadic lifestyle, Aisslinger brings up the importance of slowing down certain aspects of our daily lives to compensate. He underscores the value of "analog" activities like walking, bicycling, and the construction of simple wooden homes as useful tools for urban nomads and frequent flyers to stay connected during long periods of work and travel. Grounding both the mind and body, the concepts Aisslinger advocates are moving us closer to autarky—a model where the latest energy producing technologies empower us to grow our own food and exchange goods with complete self-sufficiency. ●

GABRIELA GOMES
Shelter ByGG

An experimental object combines sculpture, design, and architecture to form a memorable spatial experience. The futuristic, habitable module integrates sustainable materials with an understated yet youthful interior aesthetic. Intimate without feeling oppressive, the tiny shelter resembles a crimson cartoon cloud dropped from the sky. Combining sustainable solutions with themes of mobility and public space, the occupiable sculpture finds its artistic expression in the realm between the public and private.

TENGBOM ARCHITECTS
10 Smart Square Meters

This futuristic plywood dwelling provides affordable, efficient, and environment-friendly student housing. The 10 square meters unit was developed in collaboration with students from the University of Lund. Rounded doors and windows give the tiny shelter a whimsical and youthful quality. Built-in furniture, storage, and hammocks make the most of the compact footprint while maintaining an airy and cheerful atmosphere. The lightweight unit can be easily transported and reconfigured to form an individual residence or social collective comprised of multiple units.

Kul med nya former på öppningar?
Trä och glas följt åt och ger nya sätt
att forma huset. Takvalven gör det
lättare med runda hörn på
öppningar. Karmstil är överflödiga.

Smått betyder inte trångt, här bor en
protetisk student som har höga krav och
vill få ut maximalt av sitt studiemedel.

These bespoke tents combine the love of the great outdoors with glamorous amenities for the less rustically inclined. Without sacrificing comforts, the high-end tents strike a balance between aesthetics and function. The recyclable, durable, organically-shaped structures merge ecological values with luxurious design. Complete with outdoor patios, these mobile units minimally impact the landscape. Four interior design concepts offer contemporary color schemes, furniture, and accessories to fit a range of style preferences. Youthful and casual, the tents' visual and atmospheric image evolves from day into night. The iconically shaped units become translucent lanterns after dark—beacons of comfort, design, and ecology.

A small-scale retreat for a violinist and her young son values atmosphere over ostentation. The simple, modern house was fabricated offsite and delivered to the property in its completed state. Occupying a thin band of greenery between sections of cornfield, the structure responds to the two-sided condition of the landscape. Working within the roadway shipping limitations, the residence still achieves a high-end housing solution. The prefabricated house thoughtfully adapts to a modest budget as it fuses elegance with economy.

TOMAKAZU HAYAKAWA ARCHITECTS
_CC4441_

Tastefully repurposed shipping containers establish two distinct workspaces for two partners. The stacked and shifted containers house an office in one and a small gallery in the other. An elegant take on an industrial structure, the resulting spaces exude a contemporary sensibility and a strong relationship to the outdoors. The dark exteriors find balance with the crisp white interiors. These efficient structures can be reconfigured or recycled in response to future conditions and changes in ownership.

A recycled, royal blue shipping container now acts as a charming guesthouse. Fitted with a fully functional bathroom and grey water system, the container also opens up to the surrounding landscape with sliding glass doors and floor-to-ceiling windows. A green roof insulates the structure, while generous overhangs shade the outdoor patio. The open interior, clad in bamboo plywood, stages a youthful and comfortable space for relaxation. Brimming with sustainable strategies, the guesthouse repurposes a one-way container to give it a new and permanent use.

LOT-EK
MDU, Mobile Dwelling Unit

A single, red shipping container transforms into a mobile dwelling unit. Cuts in the metal walls of the container generate extruded sub-volumes, each encapsulating one living, working, or storage function. When traveling, these sub-volumes retreat to form a flush exterior surface for worldwide standardized shipping. When in use, all sub-volumes are pushed out, leaving the interior of the container completely unobstructed and all functions accessible along its sides. Fabricated entirely out of standard and plastic coated plywood, the interior of the container, sub-volumes, fixtures, and furnishings all enjoy a unified finish treatment. The live/work dwelling, conceived for individuals moving around the globe, becomes its transient owner's constant companion.

BONNIFAIT+GIESEN
Port-a-Bach Container House

This redesigned shipping container acts as a playful, mobile shelter. The thoughtfully designed, compact, and flexible dwelling can easily be moved from site to site. Unfolding in a matter of minutes, the closed container transforms into an open multipurpose unit. Fold-down façade panels double as outdoor decks, while glass doors connect the interior to the landscape. The unit includes bunk beds, a family living area, and a generous bathroom. Modest but charming, the dwelling sparks an active and adaptable approach to living alongside nature. The nomadic retreat affords a unique and open-ended opportunity to continuously reframe one's relationship to the wild.

BRUEDERS
The Grand Market Hotel

Built for the international Theater der Welt festival, a temporary hotel suite marks an inventive collaboration between the designers and Raumlaborberlin. The paired-down interactive space situates inside a constantly changing, scenic, urban location. Offering event guests a unique experience, the freestanding room appears within the fruit and vegetable section of a wholesale facility. The vast warehouse space, chosen for its nightlife, awakens when the sun sets. Not a place for people looking to relax, the shelter instead provides a protective framework to view the urban choreography within the space. The hotel itself consists of three recycled, two-square meters skylights and a bed. From this partially exposed vantage point, daring guests confront a new view of the city complete with behind-the-scenes looks at restaurants, storefronts, and weekly markets.

SIBLING
Sleeping Pods

Impermanent sleeping quarters temporarily domesticate a large warehouse space. A hybrid of work and living quarters combine to create a live-work dynamic akin to a commune. Exploring an alternative living arrangement that falls outside of the increasingly unaffordable housing market, the multi-purpose plywood shelters reactivate a previously dormant building. Each den reflects its inhabitants' personalities.

The extroverted structure features a platform that runs around the den's perimeter. This platform provides a place for performance, prompted by the positioning of a built-in wardrobe, desk, and shelving units on the raised ground. The more introverted structure integrates two solid walls that shield the view. Both habitats find a common ground in a shared informal living area located in between each module.

MONICA FÖRSTER
Clouds

Just as its name suggests, this cloud-like, portable room easily transports from place to place. The inflatable room used for meeting, resting, or concentrating collapses into a normal-sized sports bag. Simulating the feeling of being among the clouds, the hideout is made from a transparent-white nylon material. The design uses a minimum of material and generates a minimum of waste. A quiet fan inflates the space in just four minutes and keeps the space inhabitable for as long as needed.

FREYJA SEWELL
Hush

At a time when it has never been easier for us to connect, this project provides a much-needed space for the moments in which we want to withdraw. This hideout provides a nurturing and quiet enclosure for personal retreat. A light grey industrial felt on the outside reveals an inviting plush crimson red on the inside. This supple interior offers a dark, hushed, and organic nook for respite. Luxurious, personal, and organically shaped, the escape pod can be readily used in a busy hotel, airport, office, library, and other densely populated areas.

Open 24 hours a day, 7 days a week, this striking undulating building provides a futuristic environment for collaboration and creativity. The co-working space hosts a range of global companies from SurveyMonkey to Foursquare as well as a spectrum of creative agencies and homegrown innovators. The winding halls and unconventional layout promote the exchange of ideas and industries. Understanding the power of intelligent architecture and curation to support creative entrepreneurship, this home away from home brings entrepreneurs and creative businesses together in the pursuit of great work.

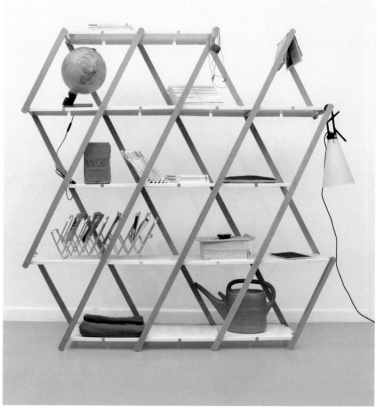

This minimalist shelving system is the result of a series of explorations with braiding techniques. Delving into themes of lightness, flexibility, and simplicity, the chosen braiding technique synthesizes all of these aspects. The resulting design of the shelving system derives its logic from the principle of a scissor grid with extended axes that make room for the shelves. This gridded extension creates a superimposed image of adjustable diagonals which can be fixed in a number of different positions. The scissor grid system can also be flat-packed while moving or for distribution.

STEPHANIE HORNIG
Camp Daybed

Sofa by day and sleeping bag by night, a simple furniture concept questions the excessive upholstery and hard shells of traditional sofas. The sleeping bag with legs provides ample space for sleeping while integrating a deep seat for use as a daybed. A padded fabric hangs over the low backrest and tightens with rubber bands. Similar to a tent, attached back pockets store unused pillows or magazines. The duvet cover can be easily removed and washed. Retaining the mobile spirit of the sleeping bag, a dismountable frame makes the daybed simple to transport.

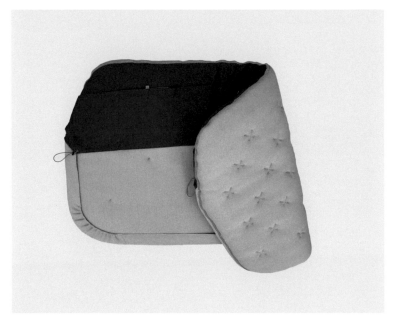

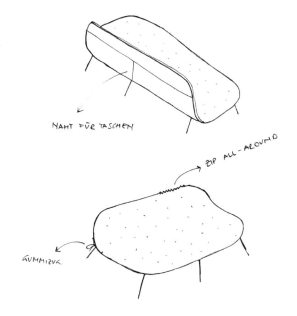

METEOR COLLECTIF
Pumpipumpe

Order your stickers online, stick them on your mailbox, and let your neighbors see what things they can borrow from you. The currently free, non-profit program promotes community interaction. As a simple and easy tool to manage the exchange of consumer goods, the straightforward graphic system supports the borrowing and lending of useful items we seldom use. Whether temporarily exchanging a drill, bicycle, or something more eccentric, the volunteer-based program activates the good neighbor in all of us.

INFLATE
Suffolk Pod

This five square meters shelter represents the first permanent use of the AirClad system. The structure, made from translucent AirCells, brings generous amounts of light into the interior. This repeating system of one meter wide cells is fixed onto a structural frame. These cells then inflate, adding to the structural integrity of the building as well as enhancing the overall insulation of the space. Embedding notions of both prospect and refuge, floor-to-ceiling glazing and a built-in door finish off the front of the experimental structure.

KENGO KUMA & ASSOCIATES
Casa Umbrella

This new type of temporary house utilizes readily available materials to form a lightweight, adaptable shelter. Comprised out of a network of assembled umbrellas inserted into an icosahedron structure, the easy-to-carry and foldable structure effectively keeps out the rain. The connection detail of the umbrellas supports changes in layout, as a new space can be defined by simply opening a different umbrella and fastening the zipper. The desired space defines the size of the umbrella needed—a few umbrellas can produce a small roof or a partition, while fifteen umbrellas can create a complete shelter. A useful shelter for a rainy day, the geometric structure zips open to welcome in the sunlight and gentle breezes during milder weather.

ZENVISION
ZENDOME.20Home-Edition

This iconic geodesic dome represents a new concept in luxury, low-carbon living and eco-tourism. Placed on a privileged wooded site, the dome lightly touches the land. Made with locally sourced wood, the retreat features a bespoke camouflage outer membrane to help the structure blend into its surroundings. Classic furniture imbues the interior with a charmingly retro atmosphere. Wastewater treatment, energy efficient appliances, and a wood pellet stove all work together to stage a memorable and sustainable getaway.

JOHN LOCKE
Inflato Dumpster

An inflatable classroom resides inside of a repurposed dumpster. The installation hosts a number of workshops and events. Built with a crowd-funded budget of just 3,685 euros, the curious metallic project behaves as a successful neighborhood activator. The inflatable rooftop creates a vaulted ceiling space for the interior, abstracting and elevating the spatial qualities within. This rooftop canopy features a geometric pattern that generates atmospheric lighting qualities for the classroom work environment. Flexible and demountable, the classroom can come and go depending on available education programs and community interest.

THOMAS STEVENSON
Bivouac

Six artist-built lean-to tents and one canteen form an unusual urban camping experience for small groups of participants. The quirkily angled tents occupy the roof of an industrial or commercial building. Thomas Stevenson, the artist and host of the metropolitan camping ground, plays the role of camp counselor and park ranger. Leading campers in preparation for communal meals and other activities, Stevenson guides his guests in a gradual process to disconnect from the overly connected world all around. Participants must bring a sleeping bag and food to share, and are requested to leave all electronics behind.

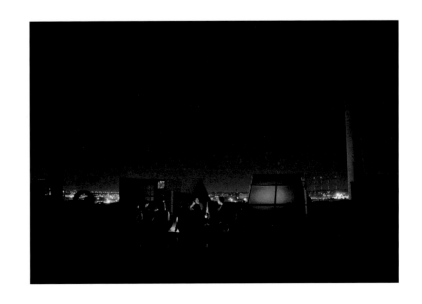

ADRIAN LIPPMANN
FoldFlatShelter

Novel and distinct, a geometric tent-like structure presents an imaginative prototype for disaster housing. The mobile unit, developed using foldable elements, integrates a weather-proof and fire-resistant exterior shell. Two interpenetrating truncated pyramids make up the basic structure of the compact shelter. Built from light-weight, long-lasting composite panels, the freestanding modules can be shipped lying flat and assembled by two people in five hours. The efficient design can join with wall or roof elements to gain floor area as needed. Flexible, efficient, and aesthetically daring, this unique system elevates the shelter solutions available to those displaced by natural disasters.

ALLERGUTENDINGE
Spirit Shelter

Inspired by the dream of Arcadia, this modest yet emotive hideaway affords its single guests the chance to live in harmony with themselves and the surrounding nature. Similar to the idea of Arcadia, the bright two-story wooden shelter consists of two main parts. The research section provides tools to discover the physical world and the wilderness, while a sleeping section offers space for meditation and self-exploration. In order to ensure that you find your own personal Arcadia, the shelter is designed as a modular system that can be disassembled and transported to any location.

GARTNERFUGLEN ARCHITECTS & MARIANA DE DELÁS
Grooming Retreat

Learning from the importance and formality of horse grooming before and after riding, this delicate shelter focuses on the ritual of cleansing both mind and body. The elevated sanctuary helps its occupants regain the time devoted to oneself without remaining too sheltered from the natural environment. Set at the center of a barley field surrounded by indigenous bushes and wild olive trees, the translucent structure grants its guests a panoramic view of the Mediterranean Sea. The meditative outlook quiets the mind, inspiring the users to reconnect with themselves and the world around them.

A modular, stackable sleeping cell provides imaginative temporary housing for festival-goers. Built into honeycomb-shaped communities, the Belgian design quickly stacks into four levels. The system achieves an incredibly small footprint while housing 50 guests in king-sized beds. Installed in the middle of the action, the social layout includes a cozy bed that can be folded into a lounge seat. The repeating design includes spaces for interaction, relaxation, safety, and community. Developed as an integrated product-service-system operated by social entrepreneurs, the sustainable design made from eco-materials also creates jobs for the mentally and economically underprivileged workforce.

BUREAU A
Monte Verita

A nomadic theater set derives its conceptual language from the play it hosts. Monte Verita, a play written by Souschiffre, depicts a utopian community in search of a new way of life in harmony with nature. Behaving as a small community in its own right, the set organizes around a sauna where the spectators can unwind and socialize before and after the show. The impromptu and mysterious set, currently traveling across Switzerland and Italy, can be dismantled in just a few hours and stored in a small truck.

SHIOGUMO
ECS-p1 – Emergency Shelter

In response to Lebanon's standing as the country with the highest ratio of refugees per capita, this emergency prototype engages a simple repeating element to form a durable shelter with surprising aesthetic quality. The robust shelter references how refugees typically build their own shelters, using common, easily accessible, and everyday objects. This minimalist yet high endurance unit engages just two components as construction materials: industrial plastic crates and plastic zip ties. Reusable and recyclable, the crate system doubles as storage units, seating, and table legs. Calibrated to perform best in hot and dry climates, the perforated crates offer improved natural lighting, ventilation, and cooling while remaining structurally stronger than conventional refugee tents.

Colorful and geometrically expressive, a reconfigurable, indoor architectural system develops flexible partitions through repetition and pattern. The double-wall corrugated cardboard system is available in 10 stock colors and custom designs. Easy to assemble, disassemble, and reassemble, the free-standing structures form spatial dividers, temporary rooms, displays, and even stage backgrounds. The tool-free assembly does not damage floors or other permanent structures, making the system a sensible and aesthetic solution for a nomadic, creative working environment.

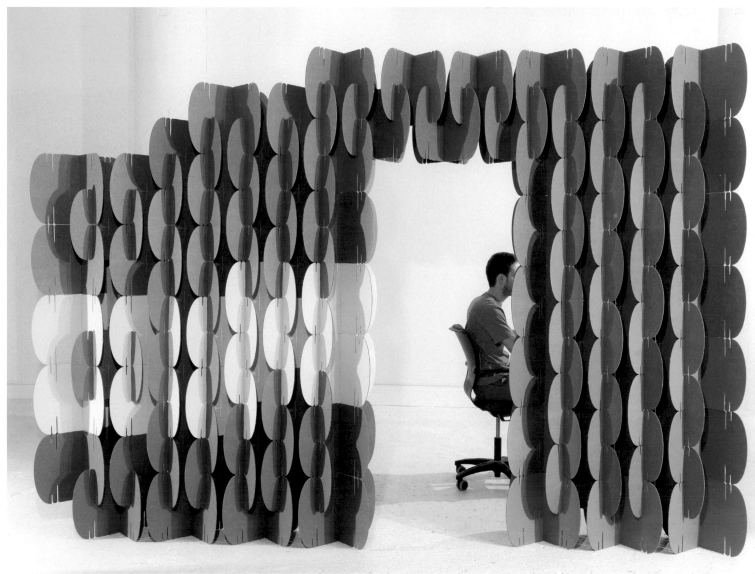

ANDREW MAYNARD ARCHITECTS
Nebula

A repurposed old school room enjoys a second life as a studio for the Art Day South artists. This project transplants the previously isolated facility into the center of Melbourne's thriving art scene. Fighting against the typical relegation of the disabled to our cultural fringes, the bright and colorful structure allows twelve artists to become active participants in mainstream life. The flexible, adaptable, safe, and inclusive project empowers the group to explore not only their own work but also the broader landscape.

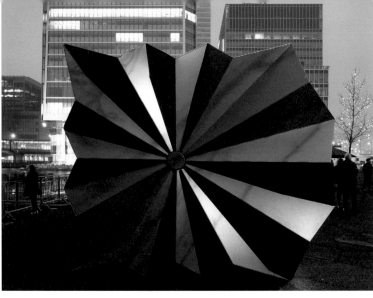

Two unique prefabricated retail kiosks sit on a landscaped waterside location within the Canary Wharf estate. These highly distinctive, sculptural kiosks provide an efficient and functional trading facility for vendors. The simple yet striking folding geometric form derives its logic from the concept of origami. Expressed as a compact, rectangular box when closed, the structure transforms when open. Folds and hinges in the steel panels allow the kiosk to contract for the night or expand into a natural canopy to serve customers during the day. The interior components easily adapt to suit the needs of individual vendors. Lightweight and resilient, the portable kiosks were tested off-site, delivered pre-assembled, and can be enjoyed in numerous incarnations and locations.

119

Mimicking the design language of the classic tangram, a Chinese game of individual triangle-derived pieces that can rearrange into various forms, this flexible modular roof structure covers a market space for the 2014 COART Festival in Lijiang, Yunnan. The flat, crimson red roof ensures the modules remain directionless, unlike typical canopies. Infinitely expandable in all directions, the spaces created underneath enjoy unified shaded coverage. The lightness of the structure allows it to almost disappear into the background while the canopy appears to float above. The long spans generate flexible open spaces on the ground with minimal obstructions.

SELGASCANO
Second Home London Office

Open 24 hours a day, 7 days a week, this striking undulating building provides a futuristic environment for collaboration and creativity. The co-working space hosts a range of global companies from SurveyMonkey to Foursquare as well as a spectrum of creative agencies and homegrown innovators. The winding halls and unconventional layout promote the exchange of ideas and industries. Understanding the power of intelligent architecture and curation to support creative entrepreneurship, this home away from home brings entrepreneurs and creative businesses together in the pursuit of great work.

Bright and understated, this refurbishment provides an alternative to the standard image of the hotel room. The rooms operate as multi-purpose spaces that combine a range of elements and materials. Reflecting the creative, raw, and surprising surroundings of East Berlin, the design re-uses and showcases salvaged materials. The layout brings together functionality and flexibility while demonstrating how to plan units for multiple uses. Furniture becomes an integral part of the design—fully connected pieces linked by function to both the space and supporting elements.

SCHEMATA ARCHITECTURE OFFICE
Paco

A white, three cubic meter large cube serves as a conceptual model to achieve a simpler way of life. The compact space provides the minimum elements needed to live a comfortable life with zero excess. Depending on the location, the unit can support a range of functions from studio to bedroom and beyond. The top of the cube cracks open along three faces, inviting the sky into the modest space. Built on a tiny footprint and with a strong relationship to the outdoors, the mobile module becomes a delicate enclosure full of light.

ARCHIPOD
Archipod Garden Office

This charming office pod provides a viable alternative to commuting to work everyday. The bubble-shaped garden office solution presents a quiet space for concentrated work. The convenient and compact workspace integrates a wraparound, semi-circular desk. Clad in red cedar wood shingles, the module stays connected to its surroundings via circular skylights and windows. A top-hinged gull-wing door swings open for entry and blends back into the shingled façade when closed. Landing somewhere between formal and informal, futuristic and quaint, the tiny structure rethinks contemporary work habits and aesthetics.

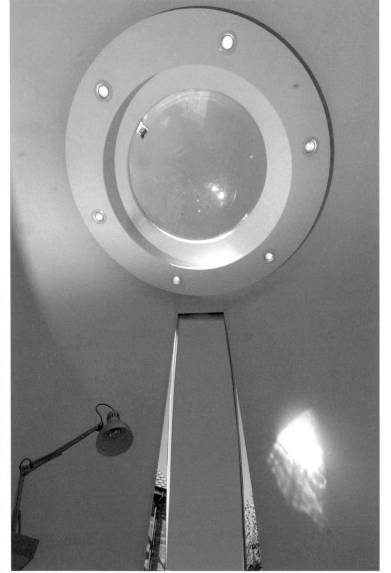

DMVA ARCHITECTEN
Blob VB3

This futuristic space egg houses all of life's bare necessities: a bathroom, kitchen, bed, lighting, and several niches for personal storage. The nose of the hideout opens automatically and functions as an impromptu porch. Supporting a variety of uses, the mobile unit can function as an office, a guest room, a reception space, a garden house, and more. The curious white egg moves easily from place to place. Well-insulated walls, an all white interior and exterior treatment, as well as the unfolding segments in the cupola and nose illuminate the interior without exposing it to direct sunlight. Unconventional and charmingly quirky, the organic shelter begs the question: which came first, the happy life or the egg?

Named after an Ancient Greek philosopher known for his ascetic life lived inside a barrel, this experimental shelter serves as a prototype for nomadic, off-grid housing. The micro unit supports a number of uses ranging from workspace to studio and weekend home. Sustainable and mobile, the tiny pitched-roof dwelling promotes a paired down approach to living without sacrificing basic creature comforts. Whether placed in a remote forest location or just next door to one's workplace, the compact mobile home thrives in any and all settings.

ARCH GROUP
Sleepbox

With the spirit that urban infrastructure should be more comfortable, this efficient sleeping compartment offers a comfortable place to rest while in transit. The streamlined and surprisingly elegant units provide instant respite without having to waste time in search of a hotel. Sleepbox grants anyone in unforeseen circumstances the chance to spend a night safely and inexpensively or simply kill a few hours without leaving luggage unattended. Solving the universal problem of delayed flights and uncomfortable waiting rooms, the small and mobile compartment can be installed right in front of the gates at the airport. Unit features include ventilation, built-in reading lamps, and outlets for charging phones and computers. Luggage fits under the bed and each bed integrates a personal nightstand. Windows are equipped with electric blinds to ensure complete privacy within inevitably public surroundings.

THOR TER KULVE
Parkbench Bubble

This semi-public inflatable cell contains the two key essentials for modern life: a usb charger and an effective form of protection against the elements. The self-sustaining piece of outdoor furniture uses a solar panel to power its inflatable bubble, ventilate the interior, and store energy for charging on the go. Questioning issues of privacy, public space, consumerism, mobility, and social behavior, this translucent and impromptu shelter highlights how much we can truly live without.

ALFREDO BARSUGLIA
Social Pool

A tiny public pool welcomes visitors passing through this remote part of the Mojave Desert. The minimalist white pool serves as a striking piece of land art, set against the desert sand. Far from the nearest road, this micro oasis can only be reached and fully appreciated after a long walk through the land. Oscillating between sculpture and bath, the pool can be used by just one group at a time for up to 24 hours. Secret GPS coordinates and a key to the pool cover are provided to curious and motivated travelers at the MAK Center for Art and Architecture in West Hollywood, California.

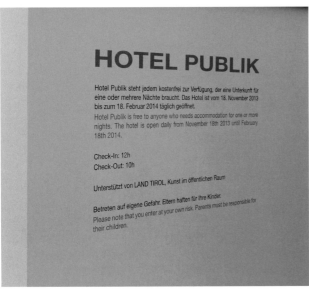

HOTEL PUBLIK

Hotel Publik steht jedem kostenfrei zur Verfügung, der eine Unterkunft für eine oder mehrere Nächte braucht. Das Hotel ist vom 18. November 2013 bis zum 18. Februar 2014 täglich geöffnet.
Hotel Publik is free to anyone who needs accommodation for one or more nights. The hotel is open daily from November 18th 2013 until February 18th 2014.

Check-In: 12h
Check-Out: 10h

Unterstützt von LAND TIROL, Kunst im öffentlichen Raum

Betreten auf eigene Gefahr. Eltern haften für ihre Kinder.
Please note that you enter at your own risk. Parents must be responsible for their children.

ALFREDO BARSUGLIA
Hotel Publik

A small, pitched roof house temporarily occupied a bustling pedestrian center in Innsbruck. Complete with heating and electricity, the compact structure fits a single bed. Operated as a hotel room, the tiny shelter is free of charge for those in need of a temporary place to stay or those curious about sleeping in a semi-public space. Guests can occupy the unit from noon until 10am the following day. Endearing in both size and spirit, the hotel cabin provides valuable respite in the heart of the city.

Urban Nomad, Co-Working Space
NeueHouse

NeueHouse, the world's first private work collective, opened its flagship location in New York City in 2013. Within just four months of opening its doors, the New York location was already oversubscribed. Co-founders Joshua Abram and Alan Murray view the power of working collectively as an exciting and tenable business model for an increasingly shifting, mobile workforce. The Neue-

unique design language balances art and industry within a series of spaces, experiences, and amenities tailored to ambitious innovators. Catering to entrepreneurs and businesses in the creative industry, the NeueHouse experience balances contemporary design and cultural programming with an eclectic and evolving membership. The diverse community of active members includes leaders in the fields of film,

House brand of workspaces, designed in collaboration with architect David Rockwell, prides itself in crafting a professional, tasteful, and social work environment for emerging and established businesses of up to 20 employees. In addition to providing a place for work, the flexible space also hosts a range of events involving luminary figures from Sir Paul Smith and Christo to Arianna Huffington. With locations in Los Angeles and London opening in 2015, the company intends to expand to 20 locations around the globe by 2020.

NeueHouse rethinks the basic workplace to craft an atmosphere for learning, inspiration, collaboration, and hospitality. The collective's

fashion, design, publishing, and the arts. Half the firms are led by women and 40 percent of the members hold passports from countries outside of the United States, with a strong presence from the United Kingdom. Global in both their outlook and professional lives, members forge an international network linking the world's creative capitals.

Meandering over five floors, NeueHouse New York occupies a renovated industrial building from 1913. With ceilings up to six meters high, the handsome space integrates the raw grandeur of the industrial setting with furnishings that reflect a non-corporate, personal, and domestic sensibility. The

138

New York location integrates a number of bespoke spaces and services including a private screening room, broadcast and recording facilities, a sophisticated art collection of work by prominent contemporary artists, and private dining rooms.

The design of NeueHouse plays a critical role in encouraging members to interact. This collection of spaces—library tables, cushioned steps for lounging, and social nooks filled with coffee tables and leather sofas—stages a welcoming environment where each member can find their ideal comfort zone. Those that use the space most productively move through different environments and experiences as their day and work dictates, sometimes working in a more social energetic space and at other times a more

quiet nook for a tête–à–tête. This flexible infrastructure will carry over to each new location, incorporating signature elements while embracing the unique nature of each landmarked space.

Demonstrating a passion for architecturally significant spaces emotionally connected to their cities, the company will soon take over the historic CBS Radio building in Los Angeles and the iconic Adelphi building in London. The Los Angeles location will repurpose a revolutionary modernist structure on Sunset Boulevard. and feature six floors of carefully integrated work and social spaces that include a 100 seat theater, outdoor cabanas, and a deck bar for Hollywood's creative class. Abram comments on the new location noting that, "Los Angeles is the next logical step in serving our culturally nomadic membership, as well as the perfect complement to New York as a

global gateway." For the London location, the bright space inside the monumental art deco blackstone will enjoy soaring two-story windows and add to the building's rich literary and artistic heritage.

NeueHouse's cultural programming draws from a cross-section of the creative arts and consists of talks, screenings, and performances by leading artists, tastemakers, and opinion leaders. "For us," the founders explain, "a great workplace must also be a powerful learning environment." The dynamic programming offers members the opportunity to come together within a fertile learning environment under the auspices of their personal interests and passions—art, music, fashion, food, etc.

NeueHouse acknowledges that where and who you sit next to influences how you work and what you work on. Even so, the founders point out that, "according to many leading academics, the best source of new ideas, inspiration, and even new gigs is more likely to come via someone with whom we have a weak connection—a person often outside of both our profession and immediate social circle." Given how our immediate network tends to replicate our own knowledge and skill set, NeueHouse instead fosters chance encounters between members. These moments of conceptual cross-pollination and outsider problem solving result in productive exchanges of insight, inspiration, and opportunities for collaboration.

As hosts, NeueHouse identifies hospitality as the key to delivering this type of supportive and serendipitous work experience. "Making people feel welcome, comfortable, and at ease immediately moves the conversation away from survival and transactions and closer to transformative encounters," note the founders. Lively conversations between fashion designers, scientists, filmmakers, technologists, and publishers generate unexpected alliances and multi-disciplinary projects that only such a diverse clientele can elicit. To become a member of NeueHouse, candidates must submit an application and be willing to be patient until their spot on the wait list materializes into actual office space. The founders describe their ideal members as "curious, open-minded, and self-aware." Requests are reviewed within the context of "maintaining an intentionally diverse and eclectic community of creative entrepreneurs."

Rather than accommodating clients in the startup industry, NeueHouse attracts an urban, independent creative class in mid-career. The company carries on a spirit of risk-taking that sets it apart from the competition while continuing to shift the paradigm of the ideal workplace. With no target users beyond established entrepreneurs who care about where they work, the NeueHouse locations act as more than just office space. Instead, each location functions as a 24/7 hub for culture, public engagement, and shared experiences to fuel curious minds. ●

The first of a series of locations for a private-membership workspace collective rethinks the contemporary office environment for today's creative professionals. Attracting a diverse workforce from the areas of film, design, fashion, art, and technology, the space accommodates solo entrepreneurs all the way up to teams of 20 people. Membership levels ranging from gallery, atelier, and studio afford businesses the flexibility to find a space, working situation, and amenities tailored to their individual needs. Suited to ambitious innovators, the new office typology spreads across five floors of a 1913 renovated industrial building. With ceilings up to six meters high, the workspace reimagines the traditional vernacular of the office aesthetic. The interior design strategy exudes a cozy familiarity with a series of living room-like spaces that embrace a non-corporate yet innovative environment for work and collaboration.

Founded in 2011, this inviting and light-filled Berlin project space reflects on alternative models for cultural, social, and economic production. The creative community mirrors the city's international and unique spirit for experimentation. Hosting both people and projects, the self-organized space builds upon the group's collective philosophy of diversity. The space separates into four distinct platforms: food, art, work, and education. Related activities in these areas range from a kitchen laboratory to co-working facilities and collaborative artist residencies. Flexible and critical, the open and vibrant think tank develops creative models for solving global issues.

BOLD DESIGN
Office On The Roof

A mini office space for a burgeoning design studio reclaims a former machine room on a Parisian rooftop. The previously unused concrete structure rests on a large terrace overlooking the city center. A minimal budget for the renovation emphasizes an economy of means. Simple, flexible, and functional, the tiny studio draws inspiration from a ship's cabin where every square inch proves valuable and optimized. Fold-out nooks and desks accommodate four workplaces for the two founders and up to two assistants.

A co-working office in a 1950s apartment bases its intriguing geometric cutout language on the seminal work of artist Gordon Matta Clark. The classic layout turned occupiable optical illusion undergoes a striking aesthetic update through a sophisticated process of subtraction. Interpenetrating oval and circular shapes are subtracted from walls to reveal visual links between previously independent rooms. By developing these apertures between one space and another, the studio achieves a collaborative atmosphere that supports interaction and dialogue between the various occupants.

This pragmatic space in Berlin functions as a combination of a Vienna-style coffee house, a library, a home office, and a university campus. The design nurtures a pleasant, positive, and upbeat co-working environment. A variety of colorful desk spaces, meeting rooms, and maker spaces are accessible to members and possible to rent for special events. The multi-purpose studio presents a range of spirited and useful workshops and courses. An in-house café with an inspired daily menu grants all areas access to quality coffee and snacks to keep focus high and bellies full.

Following the thought that designing and manufacturing go hand in hand, a fab/lab workshop keeps the creative design process visible. The space physically interprets the innovation process and the tools available. A central zone, dedicated to collective design, branches into peripheral mini-workshops that shape the different project production phases: rapid prototyping, demo and assembly, digital measurements and tests, material resource centers, and image processing. A wall of books provides technical help and creative inspiration while an alcove houses a small modular room for relaxation and discussion. As the design process requires constant interfacing between the conceptual, technical, and aesthetic dimensions, the workspace allows for the concentration of brainstorming, experimentation, and production to occur on the same topography.

A pop art illustration of a black and white office comes to life in this whimsical and surprisingly functional window display. The highly curated and eye-catching environment activates its office space more effectively while creating a compelling new display for its window treatment. Engaging passersby, the playful graphic installation choreographs a surreal monochromatic pop-up workspace that collapses distinctions between 2D and 3D space. The display, constructed entirely out of paper and card stock, features graphic cutouts of the furniture staples found in a classic office: filing cabinet, typewriter, indoor plant, and more. Through this curious lens, the public can peek into the agency's life and work philosophy.

REAL LIFE
CREATIVE TEAM
AT WORK

Installation design by **EMILY FORGOT** and **LAURIE D**
In collaboration with **WIEDEN+KENNEDY** reallifewk.com

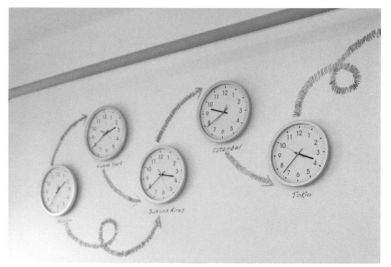

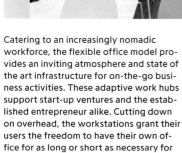

Catering to an increasingly nomadic workforce, the flexible office model provides an inviting atmosphere and state of the art infrastructure for on-the-go business activities. These adaptive work hubs support start-up ventures and the established entrepreneur alike. Cutting down on overhead, the workstations grant their users the freedom to have their own office for as long or short as necessary for the task at hand. Multiple urban locations across South America offer inviting spaces that promote a focused work environment and collaboration. The office hubs merge a professional work environment with a low-key café culture. Monthly membership includes access to work stations, Wi-Fi, meeting rooms, unlimited café beverages, and communal bicycles.

Supporting a community of creative freelancers, entrepreneurs, and small companies, this successful coworking model continues its rapid spread across Asia. The initial iteration of these elegant and welcoming creative work spaces began in Wan Chai, followed by the recent opening of two more locations in Hong Kong and Bangkok. This handsome Bangkok location, known as The Hive Kennedy Town, extends over a single 557 square meters warehouse floor space. The layout is divided into one third open plan, one third offices, and one third meeting rooms, studios, and storage spaces. Bright, understated, and inherently flexible, the office space suits a nomadic workforce of independent creatives and collectives ranging in size from 1 to 22 persons.

Nomadic Entrepreneur
by Pieter Levels

Netherlands native Pieter Levels packed up his life in Amsterdam in April of 2013 to pursue his burgeoning career as a startup mastermind. Working predominately across Asia, Levels relies on nothing more than the contents of a single backpack to support his nomadic lifestyle. In 2014, he announced his plan to develop and launch 12 startups in 12 months. A man of his word, the young programmer continues his rapid streak of innovation and prototyping from cafés and co-working spaces across Southeast Asia.

After completing his master's degree at the Rotterdam School of Management, Levels started a YouTube channel—*Panda Mix Show*—for electronic music. The channel's popularity and financial success led to Levels feeling isolated as he worked on the project from home while all his friends now held day-jobs. This feeling of restlessness inspired him to sell the majority of his belongings and book a one-way ticket to Asia. Since then, Levels has hopped from country to country, maxing out his 30-day travel visas as he goes. Levels comments on his life on the road explaining that, "It's become more normal for me to travel than not to. Airplanes have become akin to buses for me."

Levels's ambitious 12 startups in 12 months project has kept him busy and financially stable during the course of his recent travels. A few of these online products include the straightforward

Play My Inbox and the motivational *Go Fucking Do It*, where you name your goal and pay Levels an agreed upon amount if you fail to complete it. *Nomad List*, perhaps his most resourceful platform to date, provides a forum for transient workers to connect with one another. "Setting up a routine in a new place is always a challenge," Levels explains, "you need to figure out accommodations, a place to work, etc." *Nomad List* offers "crowdsourced information of the best cities to live and work remotely as well as housing and workspace tips."

Some of these startups have performed so well that they are being developed into full-fledged companies in their own right. Following the culmination of the project in April of 2015, Levels will release a mini book by the same name. This book will feature an in-depth look at each of the twelve startups "from idea, to launch, to growth." Proceeds of the book will fund Levels's next startup ventures.

With just two boxes of nostalgic items in storage at his parent's house, Levels prides himself in whittling his day-to-day possessions down to what fits inside his backpack. When discussing the challenge of what to take along versus what to leave behind he explains, "I don't really value non-functional stuff, most of the stuff I value is digitally stored. I don't even have a wallet." The few items that do make it into his backpack are predominately work related: a MacBook Pro, an iPhone, and a drone. The computer serves as his tool for creative expression. "It's what I make everything with and spend most of my time on day-to-day," he states. His more unconventional belonging, the Phantom Vision 2+ drone, gets thrown into the sky to film his shifting whereabouts.

Levels typically stays in each location for a month, taking advantage of most countries' free 30-day travel visa. Thailand's more lenient visa policies result in Levels spending more of his time there. Speaking about visa concerns, he notes, "I wish all countries made it easier (for everyone) to travel more freely, it would make it a lot more fun and would make the world even more international."

Adapting to a constantly changing environment, Levels acknowledges the challenges such a transient lifestyle can present. "If you travel so much," Levels explains, "you lose touch of where your home is." This uprooted feeling stems from the absence of a stable constant in one's daily life. So while Levels rationally sees himself as a citizen of the world he notes that his "subconscious, emotional and biological systems" needed time to adjust. He translated these feelings of loneliness into a pragmatic solution—a chat group for remote workers and travelers called #nomads (hashtagnomads.com). The group now has 1,500 members, of which 500 people actively chat daily about nomadic life and meet up in cities when they overlap. "It's been great to feel like you're part of a greater community," Levels says.

Levels champions the value of coworking spaces to support a nomadic workforce. "Remote work and digital nomads are much bigger than the cliché 'escape your 9 to 5 and go on a beach with your laptop business,'" Levels argues. One of his favorite co-working spaces is Hubud in Ubud, Bali. Made out of bamboo, Hubud fosters a creative

With workers now competing on a global scale, Levels's approach to work is less about being unconventional and more about simply staying ahead of the curve. "If you're still competing with only people in your city or country," he points out, "you need to start thinking of what happens when someone better comes up from a different region working remotely, because it's going to happen." As many corporations now hire the best talent from wherever they might be located, Levels's flexibility makes him a prime example of what the future of employment will look like following a continued period of globalization. "Most of the world has already become the same," he reflects, "From San Francisco to Amsterdam to Tokyo, people just want to be able to buy food, have friends, build families and have fun. It's the same everywhere." ●

"From San Francisco to Amsterdam to Tokyo, people just want to be able to buy food, have friends, build families and have fun. It's the same everywhere."

community of reputable startups, photographers with 200,000+ Instagram followers, documentary filmmakers for National Geographic, and many more. Levels's recent popularity, however, has made co-working spaces less and less viable for getting work done. "Since the 12 startups thing, everybody wants to talk to me," Levels ruminates, "and that's really nice, but it makes it impossible for me to code." He now opts for coffee shops with standing desks or simply working from home.

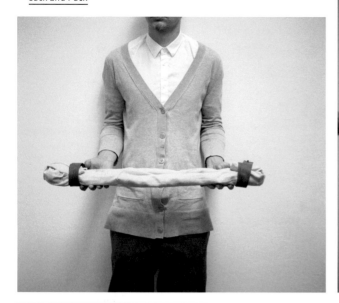

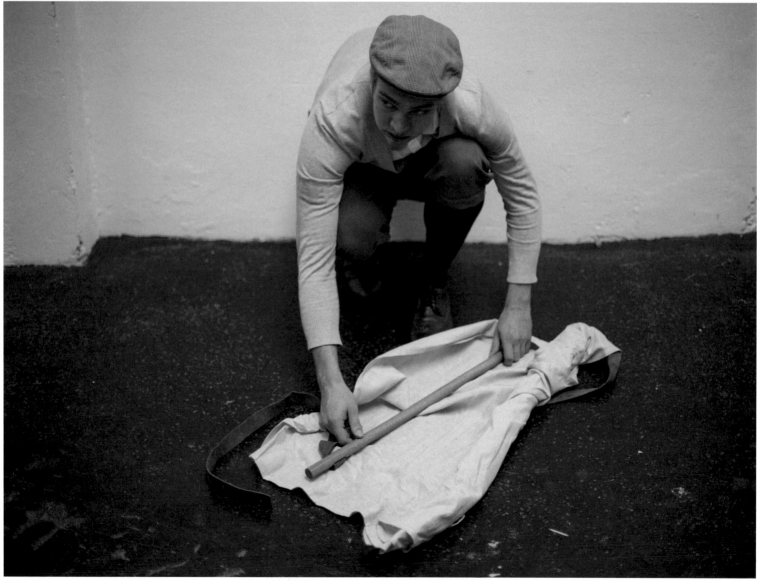

This minimalist product for the contemporary wanderer channels the romantic images found in children's books and stories such as The Adventures of Tom Sawyer. Inspired by the classic knapsack where a piece of cloth is tied to a fishing rod or tree branch, the limited edition design takes this stereotypical image and tailors it into a functional object of desire for adults. The basic materials for the product include oiled oak, browned steel, leather, and linen. A sentimental reminder of our youthful dreams, this simple knapsack reawakens our inner wanderlust. Holding just the most elementary belongings, the limited carry-on frees us up to embark on an authentic and adventurous journey.

BJARKE FREDERIKSEN
Nomad

Multi-purpose yet minimalist, this flexible furniture piece morphs from a knapsack or travel bag into a blanket and even a chair. The adaptable system works with fabric and wooden dowels to produce a product that can carry a human or a human can carry. Choreographing a responsive relationship between product and user, the ingenuity of the piece of furniture resists the traditional solution of addressing static functions. Instead, the product's inherent ambiguity questions what objects we choose to own—a contemporary reflection on form, function, material, craft, and time.

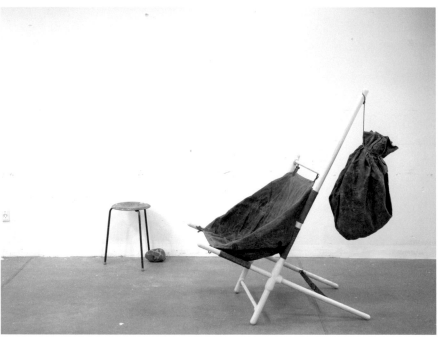

163

JODY KOCKEN
Urban Picnic

A modern version of the knapsack empowers the adventurously inclined to easily bring along both the picnic and picnic blanket on shorter or longer excursions. Balancing over one shoulder, the stick and cloth tie into an efficient bundle. The fabric of the sack doubles as a tablecloth, inspiring casual picnics along the way. Inside, the bundle holds custom stackable tableware for storing all the accoutrements needed to stage the perfect picnic.

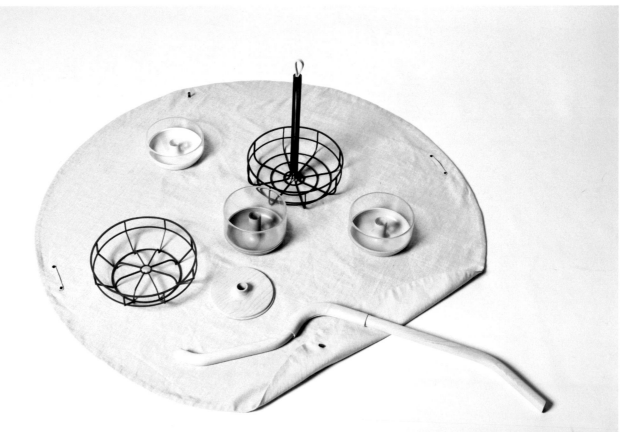

Located in a tidal creek on the Beaulieu River in the New Forest National Park, a floating wooden egg functions as a live/work laboratory. The laboratory's presence in this serene location, once home to the artist Turner for a year, raises awareness of the eroding British coastline and rising sea levels caused by climate change. The interior subdivides into a cozy living/sleeping space with a circular skylight and separate cooking/washing areas. A photovoltaic panel and a small charcoal-burning stove provide power for the shelter. Two plywood keels below the waterline allow the structure to rest on the mud at low tide. Constructed by a local boat-builder entirely from timber, the inside is built from a recycled shed while the exterior integrates a cladding of red cedar wood strips. This exterior cladding remains untreated to show evidence of weathering and decay over time.

A micro-circular dwelling provides a low-cost solution for empowering people to move around, change their whereabouts, and live in various environments. The round unit supplies space for a single nomadic occupant. Mobile on both land and water, the capsule can be moved slowly by pushing it like a wheel or walking inside or on top of it. On water, the unit can be rowed, moved by a kite, or hooked onto a larger vessel. The industrial pod rests on one flat side and can be anchored in lakes, rivers, harbors, or at sea. On land, the flexible shelter meanders across cities, fields, and forests alike.

SEALANDER
Caravan & Yacht

A few adjustments transform this shelter from a caravan into a yacht. On land the simple structure acts as a refuge, bedroom, and galley. On water, the same hideout becomes a bathing platform, pleasure boat, and meditative oasis. A one-piece, waterproof hull formed of plastic embeds picture windows to grant an unobstructed view of ever-changing land and seascapes. True to its name, the Sealander unites the high quality aesthetics of boat-building with the flexibility of a mobile home. The dynamic and modern design expresses lightness and agility. The interior combines contemporary stainless steel and plastic with traditional wood and leather to create a unique design language. Flexible both inside and out, the interior benches convert into a spacious bed. With the sunroof closed, the land and water vehicle transforms into a safe haven sheltered from wind and inclement weather.

A whimsical, multi-level floating structure features a sauna, cabin, sun deck, diving tower, and a place for barbecuing. Part raft and part boat, the modest retreat introduces four hammocks across the different levels. The sauna interior welcomes up to 13 people at a time for relaxation. The heat from the sauna stove also warms the shower and cabin space. Perfect for winter or summer getaways, the floating sauna provides the ultimate infrastructure for concentrated respite amidst ever-changing scenery.

STUDIOMOBILE & PNAT
Jellyfish Barge

In a world where resources are increasingly scarce, a floating barge responds to such pressing issues of how to continue food production, access fresh water, and find new areas for cultivation. Designed and developed by a multidisciplinary team of architects and botanists, the aquatic agricultural greenhouse produces food without consuming land, fresh water, or energy. Resembling the shape of a jellyfish, the wood and glass structure addresses communities vulnerable to water and food scarcity. The prototype, built with simple technologies and recycled materials, presents a low-cost solution to respond to many of the most pressing environmental issues of our time.

An elevated yurt brings adventure to your doorstep. Inspired by the classic yurt, a portable structure developed by the nomadic people of Central Asia, this shelter updates the ancient dwelling and refines it for the twenty-first century. The minimalist but gracious rounded structure utilizes cutting edge design and manufacturing techniques. A compact pack size liberates valuable storage space when the yurt is stowed away, while the lightweight construction allows for easy transportation by car. Whether setting up basecamp in the mountains or pitching a guest bedroom in the garden, moving houses has never been so simple or looked so elegant.

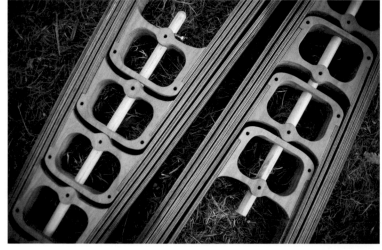

JOHN PAANANEN
Suburban Tipi

Fusing the nomadic home designs of the yurt, tipi, and igloo, this unusual retreat grounds its methodology within a set of suburban values, materials, and construction methods. The partially translucent and undulating tipi features an exterior of durable PVC siding. Inside, the curved interior is finished with plastic laminate flooring, a recessed concrete fire pit, carpet tile, and paneled walls with a photorealistic mural of a tranquil forest. The hideout questions our everyday habits, lifestyles, and values. Intimate and essential, the modest dwelling reframes one's relationship to both nature and civilization.

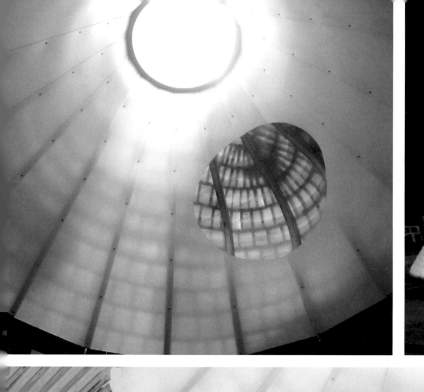

Part sunscreen part hideaway, this tactile tent behaves as a poetic retreat after a hectic day. The nomadic design reinterprets the traditional Indian tepee into a conical shape with a folding grill. Whether placed in the home or in the garden, the tranquil translucent interior makes space for one's mind to wander. The basic structure's twelve sails are made of extremely durable Tyvek material that can be quickly attached or removed with the use of high quality snaps. By attaching the sails, the occupant can decide whether the shelter stays fully closed, partially open, or even completely transparent. The number of installed sails defines how wind and light pass through. The wooden structure's flexible crossbars allow the tent to change its size with a single hand movement.

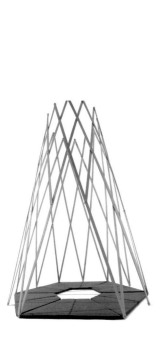

ARCHINOMA
Y-BIO Seaside Camp with Aroma Steam Bar

These pyramidal structures provide informal relaxation space and shelter along the seaside. The structures require no foundation footings, ensuring simple assembly.

Only hand powered tools are required to put together the ultra-strong tetrahedral modules. These adaptable modules can be placed on any side or hung upon any

pivot. Perfect for nomadic camping and retreat, the different units host party and social spaces as well as areas for massage, rejuvenation, and cooking. Parts of the

modules can be left open or covered with tarps to promote an unobstructed relationship to the outdoors.

ANDREA ZITTEL
Wagon Station Encampment

This futuristic encampment consists of 10 A-Z Wagon Stations, a communal outdoor kitchen, open-air showers, and composting toilets. Open to anyone with an affinity for the artist's mission in the high desert, the adaptive temporary housing hosts other artists, writers, thinkers, hikers, campers, and those engaged in other forms of cultural or personal research. The intimate community of silver pods develops a striking formal relationship with the dramatic Joshua Tree landscape while applying a light touch upon the sensitive site. Reservations can be made for one or two week visits during the open seasons each spring and fall. While free of charge, all guests must participate in the communal morning work hour known as the "Hour of Power."

V9
The Place Beyond the Rhine

A modest forest hut near a historic eighteenth century town blurs the boundaries between life and art. Designed as a distinct counterpoint to the town's prescribed paths and traditions, the rustic cabin stages a creative space free from historical constraints and societal expectations. The slightly ramshackle and compact structure calls for a more stripped down lifestyle where only the bare necessities remain. An outdoor fire pit draws social gatherings and happenings to this tiny retreat, generating a supportive space for creative outlet and collaborative thinking.

DANIEL CABEZAS LÓPEZ
Villa Ardilla

Colorful and compact, a transitional cabin adapts to the aesthetic needs of its temporary occupants while responding to its local context. The nine square meter volume divides into a lower living area and an upper bedroom level. A large window in the living room illuminates the interior, optimizes resources, and frames an impressive forest vista. The intimate sleeping area above features a generous skylight that enhances the experience of living in the treetops. Built out of materials scavenged from the junkyard, the impermanent module requires no foundation. Perched lightly on struts over the site, the cheerful hideout offers a temporary solution to get away from it all.

Located amid the historically significant former artist colony Mathildenhöhe, the International Summer School and Festival for Future Modes of Living Together occupied an experimental structure on an underused plot of the Osthang. The summer school and festival, set inside a bright and pragmatic space, brought together knowledge and experience from architecture, social and political science, economics, activism, and art. Teaching avant-garde building techniques from around the world, a team of international designers worked with 69 students. The three-week workshop explored how to build for the community by building communally.

A striking mobile shelter offers refuge and respite in both urban and rural contexts. Intended to enrich the experience of the suburbs of Bordeaux, the unusual communal dwelling introduces a provocative and unfamiliar experience right next door to daily life. Part of a series of suburban shelters, the alternative hideout comfortably accommodates up to nine guests. The structure stands as a visual hybrid between a twisting tree trunk and a piece of industrial machinery. The cozy wooden interior and studded exterior allows the unexpected off-the-grid retreat to remain on the experiential edge between art and architecture.

Similar to nature, the urban metropolis presents a diversity of landscapes and territories favorable for adventure and exploration. Part of a suburban shelters project, this intriguing series of yellow triangular hideouts stage a break from everyday life while staying just next-door. The series of micro habitats form an unusual star formation that inspires both individuation and interaction. Housing up to eight guests, the tiny shelters encourage visitors to huddle around the campfire and underneath the stars—an immersive forest experience just a stone's throw away from the city.

Lifted onto the south face of Mount Elbrus, the highest peak in Europe, the completely prefabricated and modular mountain hut holds fifty beds for adventurous travelers. The striking capsules create an environmentally sensitive hideout to comfortably endure the mountain's treacherous weather conditions. Engaging a high-tech construction process, the extruded rounded shelters enlist quality materials to form an efficient outer shell. This durable exterior skin showcases an intricate red and white pattern, adding to the capsules' futuristic appearance against the formidable moutainscape. The layout consists of two sleeping zones of stacked bunk beds, a living room and guardian room, a communal dining space and kitchen, as well as a reception space and bathrooms.

PROCESSCRAFT
Lookout

This mirrored, stainless steel cube stages the ultimate room with a view. Part of a national park project in Scotland, the reflective lookout was built on a budget of just 6,804 euros by two architecture students. The hideout camouflages itself amidst the scenic landscape, reflecting the rich green mountains. Disappearing and reappearing from view as visitors move towards the object, the structure incorporates two seats to host up to three guests. These warm, wooden seats contrast with the reflective exterior treatment as they frame intimate views of the landscape. Built by hand over two months, the outdoor folly incites a sense of wonder as it recontextualizes the world around.

Digital Nomad
by Jan Chipchase

Author, adventurer, product designer, and global entrepreneur, Jan Chipcase continues to redefine the possibilities of the mobile worker. A citizen of the world for the last 15 years, Chipchase goes where the projects take him. The culturally astute businessman negotiates upwards of 40 cities a year, answering pressing branding and research questions from his Fortune 500 clientele.

In April of 2014, Chipchase founded Studio D—a nomadic research, design, and strategy group. Tackling a wide scope of projects, some of Studio D's services include interaction design, corporate and public policy strategy, and brand positioning. "A good client comes to us with a single question and absolute trust that we can figure out the best way to answer it," says Chipchase. "We charge a lot, and work our asses off in the service of that question," he adds. The office-less studio prides itself in pop-up

workplaces. This no-strings-attached philosophy affords the company a rare opportunity to set up shop in a downtown loft in New York City one month and move on to a rural mountain retreat in Myanmar the next. Occupancy in these diverse locations can range from just a few days up to six weeks. The many experiences and cultural intelligence that Chipchase has gathered as a professional nomad can be found in his numerous writings about mobile working. His latest writing project, *The Field Study Handbook,* is slated for completion by the end of 2015.

With no full-time employees, Studio D assembles effective teams on an as-needed basis. These bespoke teams respond to the evolving demands and shifting cultural landscape of a given project. Helping clients figure out what is happening on the ground, teams of two to three fly in and are then supported by six to eight locals. "You are only as good

In addition to the D3 Duffel, Chipchase brings along another travel accessory of his own design—the Raw Utility Pouch. The pouch, made from the same cuben fiber material as the D3 Duffel only inverted, was developed for carrying important paperwork and contracts in monsoon environments. Tested widely in dusty salt-flats and insect-infested rain forests, the water resistant pouch provides a durable and thin container for safely transporting US letter-sized documents through treacherous conditions. The simple pouch develops a handsome patina over the course of its travels.

The principles of the D3 Duffel influences Studio D's "no wheels" policy on luggage. "If you can't physically carry it," Chipchase muses, "then it doesn't make it on the trip." He associates wheels with overpacking which in turn leads to a less interesting and authentic journey spent moving across exclusively flat surfaces. "To take advantage of serendipity," Chipchase reflects, "travel light."

With a third to half of each year spent traveling, Chipchase skillfully balances life on the road with a life in San Francisco. His Japanese partner of fifteen years and their four-year-old daughter act as a stabilizing counterpoint to his often transient profession. Tasked with absorbing and processing large amounts of data with insight and perspective, Chipchase acknowledges the importance of downtime and supportive work atmospheres. Both the use of the flexible popup studios and carving out time for decompression off the grid before coming home create valuable transition zones between the work and private realms.

as your local crew," Chipchase explains, "I hire smart bi or tri-lingual locals everywhere I travel for work." He also runs a service called *The Fixer List*. This network consists of unusual talent hired onto projects as well as contacts for hundreds of people Chipchase has personally interviewed over the years. The Fixer List acts as a version of his personal international rolodex as he moves from place to place. "I only need a few people across timezones that I can rely on," he states, "everything else is a bonus."

Chipchase's traveling and the lessons learned from a demanding life on the road inspired the development of the D3 Duffel. This discreet, lightweight, and high endurance duffel bag fits in a business class footwell and under an economy class seat. Chipchase discusses the inspiration behind the product, explaining that, "I'm often carrying confidential material, expensive equipment, and payroll for the local crew. The D3 Duffel was born from the need to have something that stood up to the rigors of the road and wouldn't attract attention."

After a period of prototyping and gathering detailed trip reports from 10 well-travelled beta testers, the minimalist and compact duffel bag can now be purchased from his online store, SDR Traveller.

Designing a new banking service in Myanmar today and launching a new brand in Saudi Arabia tomorrow, Chipchase continues to traverse the globe, negotiate high-risk environments, and translate his experiences into a diverse set of marketable products and corporate specialties. "Everyone has an extraordinary story to tell, given the chance," notes Chipchase, "and I'm there to give them that space to think and talk." Completing two to three around-the-world tickets per year, he understands how to make the most of his time abroad and the value of coming home. Ever a believer in practicing what he preaches, Chipchase shares the rule of thumb he lives by: "Live somewhere interesting so you can learn from everyday interactions and then travel with enough time to meaningfully absorb what is going on." ●

"Live somewhere interesting so you can learn from everyday interactions, and then travel with enough time to meaningfully absorb what is going on."

POLER STUFF
Le Tente

A vehicle rooftop tent weighing just 64 kilos folds open into a cozy space for a queen-sized foam mattress. Constructed from heavy-duty waterproof canvas, aluminum poles, and a ladder, the efficient tent attaches to standard Thule or Yakima bars and can be placed on almost any vehicle. Like a snail that carries its home on its back, the white rooftop shelter accompanies the contemporary wanderer to remote destinations in challenging climates.

This canary-yellow, portable hot tub stands as the world's first hot-water-on-demand tub heated with propane, natural gas, or wood. Weighing only 23 kilos, the tub stores and travels inside a duffel bag. Perfect for warming up a crisp winter night or unwinding under the summer stars, the tub enhances any outdoor experience from the sandy beaches to the dense forests. Simple to carry and setup, the tub can accompany you wherever adventure strikes.

PORT CITY MAKERSPACE
Surf Sauna

This mobile sauna appeals to the rugged surfer who navigates the chilly and often formidable waters along the New England coast. A novel product of the Port City Makerspace in New Hampshire, the charming barrel-shaped structure stands as a labor of love, produced by a tight knit group of surfers and craftsmen. Inviting from the outside and serene in an understated manner from within, the red cedar wood structure includes a durable chassis and related hardware to move through even the most challenging off-road winter conditions. The exterior of the tiny but robust shelter includes a spot to store a surfboard or two before entering to rest your weary bones.

Compact and rugged, this all terrain and fully self-contained camping trailer began as a personal project in an effort to create a product small and light enough to be towed behind a motorcycle. The teardrop trailer proves light enough to transport easily while remaining spacious enough to house a comfortable mattress for recouping after a long day on the road. A convenient, built-in, and open-air galley sets up a visceral and lasting connection with nature. The multi-purpose trailer can fill a number of roles ranging from a sleeping compartment to a storage space and even a meal preparation and cooking station. Whether coasting down the highway for a leisurely getaway or seeking adventure in a remote destination, this trailer will help you get there, stay there, or continue exploring the vista just over the horizon.

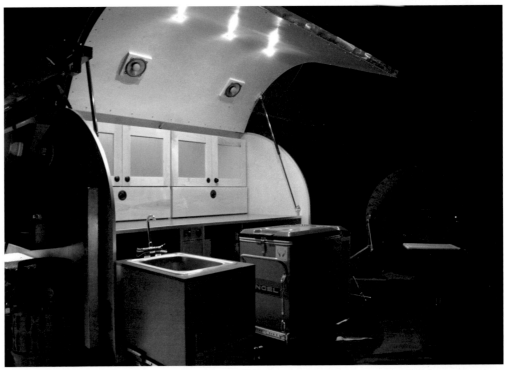

Designed and developed by a NASA architect, this nomadic trailer behaves like a spaceship for earth. The lightweight caravan, conceived as a piece of adventure equipment, stages a small interior environment ready for adventure. Combining his NASA experience with a love of the outdoors, the resulting innovative trailer presents a compact and flexible sanctuary for exploring the world. The simple, intelligent, and robust structure embeds nature and the outdoors into the rituals of daily life.

Index

PP. 184–185
ARCHINOMA
*Y–BIO Seaside Camp with Aroma
Steam Bar*
2009, Russia
Photography: Aventoza
Additional credits: Alix Shelest

PP. 186–187
ANDREA ZITTEL
Wagon Station Encampment
2012, United States
Photography: Jessica Eckert, © Andrea
Zittel, Courtesy of Andrea Rosen Gallery NY

PP. 188–189
V9
The Place Beyond the Rhine
2013, Switzerland
Photography: Daniel Künzler,
Roman Menge

PP. 190–191
DANIEL CABEZAS LÓPEZ
Villa Ardilla
2015, Spain
Photography: Cristina Beltran
Additional credits: Rosario Velasco,
Joan Sanz

PP. 192–193
RAUMLABORBERLIN
Osthang Project
2014, Germany
Photography: Kristof Lemp
Additional credits: Jan Liesegang, atelier
le balto, Collectif etc, ConstructLab,
Atelier Bow–Wow, Martin Kaltwasser,
Umschichten, m7red, orizzontale

PP. 194–195
BRUIT DU FRIGO
Refuges Périurbains – Le Tronc Creux
2013, Belgium
Photography: Bruit du Frigo, Zébra3
Additional credits: Zébra3/Buy–Sellf

PP. 196–197
BRUIT DU FRIGO
Refuges Périurbains – La Belle Etoile
2012, Belgium
Photography: Bruit du Frigo, Zébra3

PP. 198–199
LEAPFACTORY
LEAPrus 3912
2013, Italy
Photography: LEAPfactory

PP. 200–203
PROCESSCRAFT
Lookout
2014, Scotland
Photography: Ross Campbell, Processcraft

PP. 204–207
JAN CHIPCHASE
SDR Traveller, D3 Duffel
2013, United States
Photography: Jan Chipchase

PP. 208–209
POLER STUFF
Le Tente
2014, United States
Photography: Benji Wagner

PP. 210–211
THE ORIGINAL NOMAD
Collapsible Hot Tub and Heating Coil
2014, United States
Photography: Ben Werth, Evan Mitsui

PP. 212–213
PORT CITY MAKERSPACE
Surf Sauna
2013, Unites States
Photography: Amy Broman, Ross Beane

PP. 214–215
MOBY1 EXPEDITION TRAILERS LLC
XTR
2011, United States
Photography: Ashley Grimes, Moby1
Expedition Trailers LLC, Parker Grimes
Photography

PP. 216–219
GARRETT FINNEY
Cricket Trailer
2012, United States
Photography: Erin Baer

(Imprint)

The New Nomads

Temporary Spaces
and a Life on the Move

This book was conceived, edited and designed by Gestalten.

Edited by Sven Ehmann, Robert Klanten, Michelle Galindo, and Sofia Borges
Profile texts by Sofia Borges
Preface by Shonquis Moreno

Art direction by Floyd E. Schulze
Layout by Moya Ehlers
Cover photography by Malte Spindler/DIE BRUeDER © Sealander GmbH, 2014
Typefaces: Programme by Maximage
Copy-editing by Noelia Hobeika
Proofreading by Felix Lennert

Printed by Nino Druck GmbH, Neustadt/Weinstraße
Made in Germany

Published by Gestalten, Berlin 2015
ISBN: 978-3-89955-558-5

2nd printing, 2015

ALB NEW CF1